Sandra McCall's
RUBBER STAMPED

JEWELRY

NORTH LIGHT BOOKS
Cincinnati, Ohio

www.artistsnetwork.com

Sandra McCall's Rubber Stamped Jewelry. Copyright © 2005 by Sandra McCall. Printed and bound in Singapore. All rights reserved. It is permissible for the purchaser to make the projects contained herein and sell them at fairs, bazaars and craft shows. No other part of this book may be reproduced in any form or by any electronic or mechanical means including information storage and retrieval systems without permission in writing from the publisher, except by a reviewer, who may quote a brief passage in review. Published by North Light Books, an imprint of F+W Publications, Inc., 4700 East Galbraith Road, Cincinnati, Ohio 45236. (800) 289-0963. First edition.

09 08 07 06 05   5 4 3 2 1

Distributed in Canada by Fraser Direct

100 Armstrong Avenue

Georgetown, ON, Canada L7G 5S4

Tel: (905) 877-4411

Distributed in the U.K. and Europe by David & Charles

Brunel House, Newton Abbot, Devon, TQ12 4PU, England

Tel: (+44) 1626 323200, Fax: (+44) 1626 323319

E-mail: mail@davidandcharles.co.uk

Distributed in Australia by Capricorn Link

P.O. Box 704, S. Windsor, NSW 2756 Australia

Tel: (02) 4577-3555

Library of Congress Cataloging-in-Publication Data

McCall, Sandra

    Sandra McCall's rubber stamped jewelry /
Sandra McCall.

        p. cm.

    Includes index.

    ISBN 1-58180-681-7 (alk. paper)

    1. Jewelry making. 2. Rubber stamp printing. 3. Wire craft.
I. Title.

    TT212.M28 2005

    745.594'2--dc22

                  2005002779

Editor: Krista Hamilton
Designer: Terri Eubanks
Production Coordinator: Robin Richie
Photographers: Christine Polomsky, Hal Barkan, Tim Grondin

METRIC CONVERSION CHART

To convert:	To:	Multiply by:
Inches	Centimeters	2.54
Centimeters	Inches	0.4
Feet	Centimeters	30.5
Centimeters	Feet	0.03
Yards	Meters	0.9
Meters	Yards	1.1
Sq. Inches	Sq. Centimeters	6.45
Sq. Centimeters	Sq. Inches	0.16
Sq. Feet	Sq. Meters	0.09
Sq. Meters	Sq. Feet	10.8
Sq. Yards	Sq. Meters	0.8
Sq. Meters	Sq. Yards	1.2
Pounds	Kilograms	0.45
Kilograms	Pounds	2.2
Ounces	Grams	28.4
Grams	Ounces	0.04

DEDICATION

This book is for my sister Jenny.
Thanks, Jen, for helping me to see
order in chaos.

ABOUT THE AUTHOR

Sandra McCall comes to the craft arena
with an extensive art background, starting
from the moment she was first able to pick
up a pencil. A craft designer and teacher
living in northern Arizona, Sandra enjoys
finding new ways to marry basic art supplies
and rubber stamp-related products. She
attended San Jose State University,
majoring in commercial art. Sandra has
authored several books and magazine
articles, has had her work included in
multiple compilation books and has even
authored a new DVD featuring rubber-
stamped fabric projects. Her current
interests are beading, polymer clay, fabric
art and, of course, rubber stamps.

ACKNOWLEDGMENTS

No book is ever completed by the author
alone, and this book is no exception.
Thanks to everyone who worked so hard to
make this book come to life. My list of
gratitude is humongous so I'll just say thanks
to my friends, extended family, the staff at
F+W, the store owners and convention
promoters who have let me teach at their
venues, my fellow artists from whom I've
learned so much, my favorite publications
(keep them coming!), the reviewers of my
works who are so generous with their kind
words (you know who you are), and my very
understanding resource partners.

A special thanks goes to all the people who
have taken my classes along the way. Your
humor and dedication to the craft have kept
me afloat during times of doubt. I've gained
so much more from all of you than you can
imagine. Thanks, everyone!

TABLE OF CONTENTS

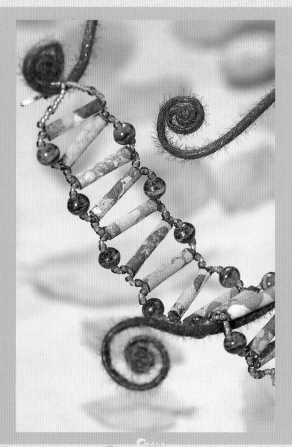

INTRODUCTION

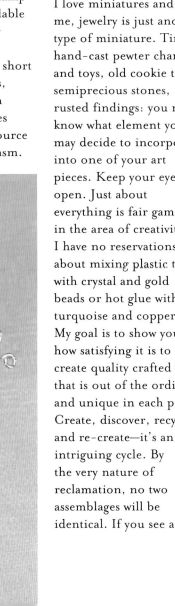

There are a lot of fabulous books on making jewelry, but not too many that bridge the gap between what I call serious jewelry and craft jewelry. The books on metal jewelry are so intense, with so much information right down to the exact temperature that the metal has to be to get a good joint, that it makes my eyes spin. Detailed information is a wonderful thing as long as all the technical verbiage doesn't scare you away from learning great new techniques.

You won't find any of that here. With this book, it is my intention, for instance, to show you how easy it is to do a simple solder even if you don't have a degree in science. I also want to give you great value for your money. This book covers a lot of materials and techniques, most of which have not been previously published. There is also a long list of resources that I think you will find useful many times over.

Rubber stamps can add so much depth and dimension to just about any art or craft. Jewelry is a particularly good partner for rubber stamp art. The designs available today in both rubber stamps and jewelry findings are nothing short of amazing. The inks, beads, wire and a ton of other craft supplies provide an endless source of ideas and enthusiasm.

Best of all, it is all so readily available. Stores, catalogs, Internet shopping—we are very lucky indeed!

I love miniatures and, for me, jewelry is just another type of miniature. Tiny, hand-cast pewter charms and toys, old cookie tins, semiprecious stones, rusted findings: you never know what element you may decide to incorporate into one of your art pieces. Keep your eyes open. Just about everything is fair game in the area of creativity. I have no reservations about mixing plastic toys with crystal and gold beads or hot glue with turquoise and copper. My goal is to show you how satisfying it is to create quality crafted work that is out of the ordinary and unique in each piece. Create, discover, recycle and re-create—it's an intriguing cycle. By the very nature of reclamation, no two assemblages will be identical. If you see a project in this book and you would like to make it but cannot find one of the exact pieces in the supplies list, look around at what you already have. I just know you'll feel far happier with the outcome if you are able to say, "Look how clever I've been with my substitutions!" Please, never let a lack of product or material be a cause for even a tiny delay in your creative endeavors.

As always, I hope you will read through the book and think about recombining all these techniques and ideas into your own unique creations. Jewelry is cool, but think beyond that as well. Think about how you can use this book to generate ideas for your altered journals, cards, gifts and even home décor. Above all, enjoy and have fun creating!

Back to Basics

The good news about all of the tools and materials used in this book is that you probably already have most of them on hand. The other good news is that even if you have none of them, most of the items that I use are very inexpensive. You don't have to buy everything on your list all at once, either. You can build your supply with the basics, then fill in the voids as money becomes available. For instance, I've been rubber stamping and bookbinding for over ten years now, and I finally bought a bone folder just last year. Before that, I used the end of a marker to flatten paper creases. Sure, some of your meaner friends will laugh at you, but don't let that stand in the way of your creativity.

Okay, back to the subject of inexpensive materials. Do buy the best tools that you can afford. Tools like crimping pliers, chain-nose pliers and wire cutters will make your crafting life so much easier if they are reliable. You really do get what you pay for in the case of these items. But, again, do not let lack of money keep you from creating.

When I started making jewelry, I used the large pliers from my garage tool box, then I graduated to a set of craft pliers and later was able to afford the better jewelry pliers one by one. They do make a difference in frustration levels. On the other hand, you can credit the lack of good tools with teaching you to use a light hand and to be as delicate with your wire as you can possibly be. I believe that it was my big, old, clunky garage tools that gave me the hand that I have today. I can still use them and not mar my wire if I need to be very careful. I must interject here that my need to be careful wholly depends on whether or not I plan to sell an item. For my own enjoyment, it is usually a matter of churning out ideas more than worrying about making a few marks on my wire. I know, I know, sacrilege!—but there you have it: the world according to Sandy!

TOOLS AND MATERIALS

On the next few pages, you will learn about the tools and materials needed to make the projects in this book. The tools you will use throughout the entire book are listed under General Tools and Materials, and the other items are broken into the particular chapter in which they are needed.

General Tools and Materials

All of these items can be found in your local craft store.

Craft knife: Get a sharp craft knife for cutting foam core, mat board, clay and glue. Be sure to change your blade often.

Craft scissors: You will need a good pair of craft scissors for cutting paper, fabric and shrink plastic, and another pair for cutting metal. I also recommend getting pinking shears for cutting zig-zagged shapes.

Heat embossing tool: Use this for drying paint and ink and for heating embossing powder and shrink plastic.

Knitting needles and dowels: You will need these in various diameters for making wire coils and jump rings.

Paintbrushes: Keep a variety of paintbrushes on hand for different purposes. You'll need several small round brushes dedicated to different paint and gloss applications, a big round soft brush for dusting off excess beads and embossing powder, and several foam brushes for applying paint to stamps and fabric.

Paper: In this book, cardstock refers to the kind of heavy-weight paper that is used to make cards.

Text-weight paper is any light-weight, inexpensive paper. Mat board is a scrap of cardboard in any weight, color or texture.

Rubber stamps: You can never have too many of these, as there are so many uses beyond stamping on paper. Stamps with a deeply etched image are versatile because they can be used for stamping in fabric and clay. To keep your stamps conditioned, always clean them with a good stamp cleaner after each use.

Embossing ink and powder: These tools create an interesting, raised image on your project. A stamp is coated with embossing ink and impressed onto a

surface, then embossing powder is sprinkled over the wet ink and heated with a heat embossing tool. This process is also called thermal embossing. I also use embossing ink as a release agent for glue stamping.

Inks: Dye ink, a vivid ink that dries quickly, works on any type of paper. Pigment ink works best for stamping on non-coated paper, as it does not dry on coated paper, or paper with a glossy finish. Solvent ink is permanent ink that works well for stamping on nonporous surfaces. Chalk ink has the resilience of pigment

GENERAL TOOLS AND MATERIALS – *From top left: heat embossing tool, water brush, markers and pens, knitting needle, paintbrush, wooden dowel, scissors, stamp cleaner, acrylic paint, ink pads, soft brush, rubber stamps.*

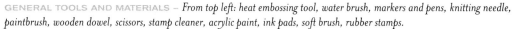

inks, yet it stamps like dye ink on most porous surfaces.

Markers, crayons and gel pens: I recommend getting a variety of gel pens, permanent markers, Galaxy markers and watercolor crayons.

Paint: Acrylic paint is a great medium for stamping on almost any surface. It is available in every color and dries quickly.

General Adhesives

The right glue for the right material will go miles in making your craft time much more pleasant.

Diamond Glaze: This dimensional adhesive can be mixed with glitter or paint for a decorative effect. It is an excellent glue and works on both porous and nonporous surfaces.

Fabri-Tac: This is my favorite glue for fabric and any other surface because it dries very quickly, is flexible when dry and really does stick!

Gem-Tac: Another favorite, this is a white glue for attaching embellishments and beads to anything porous.

Permanent adhesives for glass and metal: For glass, metal and other non-porous surfaces, I use a strong, permanent adhesive from Plaid.

Superglue: A little dab of this adhesive is great for securing knots and hardening the ends of thread and cord.

Jewelry Tools

The following tools will make your jewelry construction much more enjoyable.

Bead board: Plan out your beaded designs in advance by laying them out on a bead board before stringing them.

Bead tray: This will keep your beads from rolling off your work surface. I recommend JudiKins Snappy Tray. You can also make your own by inserting a piece of felt or velvet into a picture frame. The frame will contain the beads, and the fabric will keep them from sliding around.

Chain-nose pliers: These pliers are used for grasping wire and making small bends. The inside jaws are flat and can be smooth or have teeth.

Chasing block and hammer: These tools are used to flatten and strengthen wire that has been shaped.

Crimping pliers: These are used to secure crimp beads and tubes in place.

Round-nose pliers: These pliers have round tips and are used for making loops and bending wire.

Wire cutters: There are two types of wire cutters that I recommend.

Flush cutters are beveled on one side of the jaws and flat on the other, leaving wire with one straight side and one beveled side. Straight wire cutters are for blunt, straight cuts.

JEWELRY TOOLS – *From top to bottom: round-nose pliers, chasing hammer, crimping pliers, flush cutters.*

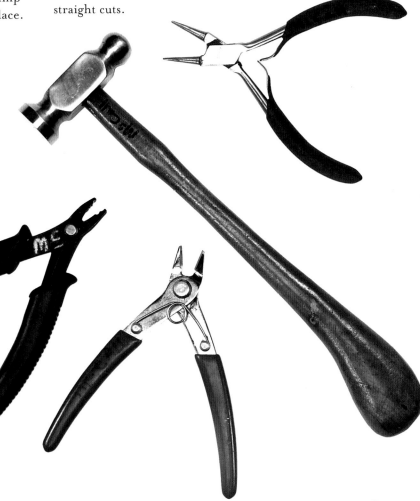

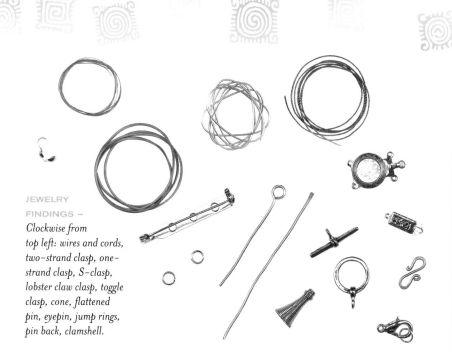

JEWELRY
FINDINGS –

*Clockwise from
top left: wires and cords,
two-strand clasp, one-
strand clasp, S-clasp,
lobster claw clasp, toggle
clasp, cone, flattened
pin, eyepin, jump rings,
pin back, clamshell.*

Jewelry Findings and Stringing Materials

The items listed here are used for connecting and stringing. They can be purchased in craft and jewelry stores, and you can make many of them yourself.

Wire: I use wire to make jump rings, headpins and eyepins, bead dangles and clasps. It comes in all colors and gauges, and the smaller the gauge size, the thicker the diameter. I use 16-gauge wire to make bangle bracelets, 18- and 20-gauge wire to make jump rings and bead dangles, 22- and 24-gauge wire for wrapping.

Jump rings: These connectors, which can be round or oval, are used to attach clasps and dangles. For instructions on how to make jump rings, see pages 18 and 19.

Clamshells: These findings are used to connect single and multi-strand wires or cords together. For more about clamshells, see page 21.

Crimp beads and tubes: These are used to attach clasps to the ends of beading wire. For more about crimp beads and tubes, see page 16.

Clasps: There are several types of clasps used throughout the book. Clasps may be attached with jump rings, crimp beads or tubes, clamshells, cones and many other jewelry findings.

Eyepins: These wire findings have a loop, or eye, at one end and are great for bead dangles. I make my own eyepins, as described on page 17, but you can also buy them.

Headpins: These are similar to eyepins, but instead of having an eye loop, they have a flat head at one end. You can make a headpin easily by crimping the end of a wire with crimping pliers. The flat end will prevent beads from sliding off the wire.

Stringing materials: For stringing beads, I recommend monofilament fishing line or beading thread, such as my new favorite, #8 FireLine. It is incredibly strong and flexible, yet thin enough to fit through small bead holes.

Pinbacks: I adhere these to the backs of my pins, then conceal them with faux suede for a finished look.

Beads

Beads, beads, beads. I love them! Here is a list of some of the beads I use in this book.

Seed beads: These beads, which measure approximately 1-2mm, are strung onto necklace cords and wires and are also used in peyote stitching.

Delicas: These beads are smaller than seed beads (approximately 1-1.5mm), but the hole is about the same so that fine beading wire can pass through several times. Delicas are great for stringing onto bead dangles and for flat beading stitches such as peyote. They are available in round and hexagonal shapes.

E beads: These beads, which are approximately 4mm, can be round, square or triangular and generally have a large enough hole for thin cord, silk ribbon or several strands of beading wire to pass through.

Bugle beads: These long, thin glass beads come in various lengths and can be round or hexagonal, as well

BEADS – *Some of the
beads used in this book,
including (from top left)
E beads, chips, tiny holeless
glass beads, and bugle beads.*

as straight or twisted. The more expensive Japanese bugle beads have smooth ends. If you buy inexpensive bugle beads with sharp edges, file the edges smooth or use durable wire such as FireLine fishing wire, beading wire or metal wire.

Chips: Irregularly cut stone beads are called chips.

Tiny glass beads: These tiny, holeless beads can be found in rubber stamp and craft stores. You can adhere them with glue, double-sided tape, ink or paint. Since they are glass, they will not melt under a heat embossing tool or in a low temperature oven.

"Get A Glue" Tools & Materials

In addition to the general tools and materials, the following items are needed for Chapter 2: Get a Glue.

Foam core: This is a layer of foam sandwiched between two layers of high-quality paper. It is available in varying thicknesses. It is the perfect surface to make beautiful, light-weight jewelry pieces.

Hot glue gun and glue sticks: These are not only great for adhesion, but in this book, I also use them for their sculptural properties. Stamping into hot glue produces very interesting results.

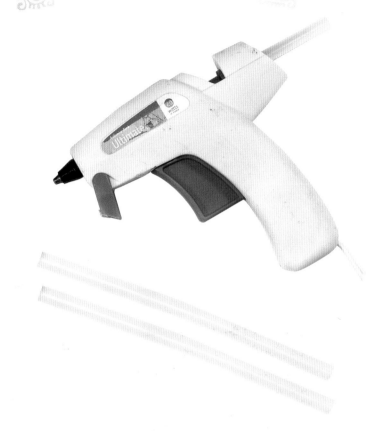

"GET A GLUE" MATERIALS – *Glue gun, glue sticks, foam core.*

"FABRIC FAVORITES" MATERIALS –
From left to right: decorated muslin, muslin, felt, faux suede, button blank. At lower right, plastic tubes, beading needle, and button blank.

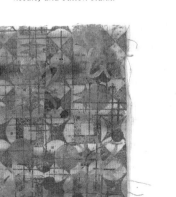

"Fabric Favorites" Tools & Materials

In addition to the general tools and materials, the following items are needed for Chapter 3: Fabric Favorites.

Buttons: These are always great embellishments for jewelry. For several projects in this book, I use button blanks, which are buttons without the jewels in them. I glue stamped and embossed images into the blank spaces. Make sure to get buttons with shanks if you are using them as pendants.

Fabric: Material such as muslin is great for stamping and decorating. I also like to cover my pinbacks with faux suede.

Plastic tubing: I love covering plastic tubes with stamped fabric. They are inexpensive, light-weight and readily available in hardware or electronics stores. Any flexible plastic tubing that can be cut with scissors will work.

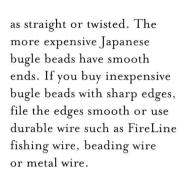

"Poly Playthings" Tools & Materials

In addition to the general tools and materials, the following items are needed for Chapter 4: Poly Playthings.

Shrink plastic: This thin, flexible plastic shrinks to about 60 percent of its size when heated. It is available in clear, semiopaque white, white, ivory, brown and black.

Polymer clay: This modeling medium must be baked in order for it to harden. It comes in a wide variety of brands and is also available in liquid form.

Hand-cranked pasta machine: Clay is rolled through this machine, which has adjustable settings for the desired thickness, to condition and flatten it.

For more information about using a pasta machine, see page 73.

Pin vise: Available in hobby shops, this is a handle with different sized chucks to hold a variety of small drill bits. You can easily make holes in baked polymer clay by turning the pin vise like a screwdriver.

Poultry lacing skewer: I use this common kitchen tool to pierce holes and drill channels in raw polymer clay. An awl or needle tool also works.

Tissue blade: This sharp, flexible blade is used for cutting thin slices in raw polymer clay.

Wet/dry sandpaper: To sand and polish baked polymer clay to a smooth finish, dip sandpaper and the finished piece into a bowl of water and sand repeatedly.

"METALWORKS" MATERIALS –
Clockwise from left: helping hands, heat sink, scrap metal, metal file, glass pieces, bezel, wire, flux.

"Metalworks" Tools & Materials

In addition to the general tools and materials, the following items are needed for Chapter 5: Metalworks.

Solder: This is a bonding medium that holds metal together. It comes in a spool that resembles wire, and melts when heated.

Flux: This is an acid that cleans metal. In order for two objects to be soldered together, flux must be applied at the connecting points on both objects. It gives the metal tooth and allow the solder to flow.

Soldering iron: This tool heats to a very high temperature and melts solder. I recommend getting an iron that has a fine tip so that you can solder tiny jump rings and other small spaces on jewelry.

Heat sink: This is a block of material, such as asbestos substitute, that will not get hot from a soldering iron, torch or piece of hot metal. It will prevent you from burning a hole in your work surface. Bricks and large tiles will not work as heat sinks. They may keep you from burning down the house, but they will crack when you put a torch to them. Ask me how I know.

Helping Hands: This inexpensive tool, found near soldering irons in jewelry supply stores and hobby shops, aids you in holding small pieces that are being soldered.

Metal file: This is used to sand down rough or sharp edges on metal.

Glass pieces: I use pre-cut glass pieces called ClinkIts! for many jewelry pieces.

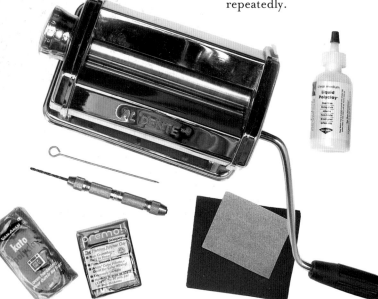

"POLY PLAYTHINGS" MATERIALS –
Clockwise from left: pin vise, poultry lacing skewer, pasta machine, liquid polymer clay, wet/dry sandpaper, polymer clay.

BASIC TECHNIQUES

You'll use the techniques featured here over and over in your jewelry making. Don't worry if something feels clumsy or difficult at first. You will be a pro once you've done it a couple of times.

INKING YOUR STAMPS

I have to say one very important thing here: Do not drag a stamp across an inkpad to ink it. This will only deposit the ink into the crevices of the stamp and brush it off the top—the very place that you want the ink. Follow the instructions below to ensure that your stamps receive ample ink coverage and make a great impression.

HELPFUL HINTS

If you have a small stamp, place your inkpad face up and tap the stamp onto the inkpad.

CLEANING YOUR STAMPS

To keep your rubber stamps in good condition, you must clean them often, as described below. I use a solvent-based cleaner called Fabric and Permanent Ink Cleaner because it removes all types of inks and acrylic paints, and it contains a conditioner that keeps the rubber from cracking over time.

▼ Place the stamp face up on your work surface and tap the inkpad lightly onto the surface of the stamp.

▼ Place the paper over the stamp and rub gently with your fingers.

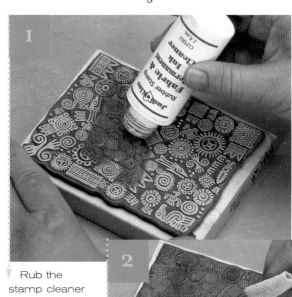

▼ Rub the stamp cleaner over the dirty stamp to saturate it completely.

▼ Rub the stamp vigorously with a terry cloth rag. The fibers from the cloth will get down into the grooves to clean the stamp more thoroughly than a smooth cloth.

TYING KNOTS

A simple square knot (A) will keep most cords secure.
If you are working with a slippery cord, or if you want to
be extra sure that a knot will stay put, a surgeon's knot
(B) will do the trick. Both are demonstrated below.

▼ **Overhand and Square Knots** – Cross the right cord
over the left cord, fold the right cord down and pull it
through the circle to make an overhand knot. For a square
knot, repeat the overhand knot in reverse, crossing the left
cord over the right cord and pulling it through the circle.
Pull taut to secure.

▼ **Surgeon's Knot** – Tie an overhand knot as you did
to start the square knot. For the reversed overhand knot,
cross the left cord over the right cord, then pull it through
the circle, back around and through the circle again. Pull
taut to secure.

USING CRIMP BEADS AND TUBES

Crimping is a technique used to attach a clasp to the
end of beading wire. All you need is a clasp, wire,
crimp bead or tube and crimping pliers. The
demonstration below shows a crimp bead, but the
same process applies when using a crimp tube.

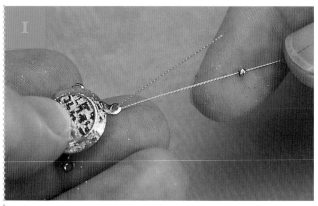

▼ Cut a piece of beading wire to the desired length.
Thread one end through the crimp bead and through
the clasp. Bring the tail of the wire through the crimp
bead. Slide the crimp bead toward the clasp.

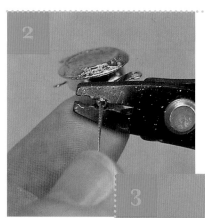

Clasp the crimp
bead in the sec-
ond section of the
crimping pliers
(the one closest
to the handle) and
smash it down.

▼ Clasp the crimp bead in the first
section of the crimping pliers and
smash down again to round the
bead and finish the crimp.

MAKING EYEPINS

An eyepin is a straight pin with a loop, or eye, at one end. Although eyepins are available in any craft store, I prefer to make them to match whatever size, type and color of wire I am using at the time. Hammering the eye is optional, but it will make the metal stronger and therefore less likely to pull apart while you are wearing your jewelry.

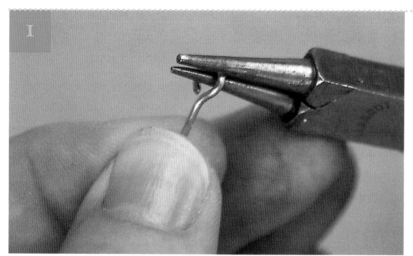

Cut a length of wire and loop one end around the tips of your round-nose pliers.

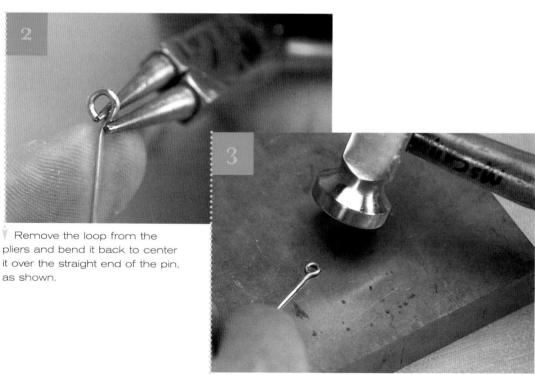

Remove the loop from the pliers and bend it back to center it over the straight end of the pin, as shown.

Place the loop on the chasing block and flatten it with the chasing hammer to strengthen it.

MAKING JUMP RINGS

Jump rings are single wire circles or ovals used to connect jewelry findings and clasps. Split jump rings are double wire circles that resemble tiny key rings; they are also used as connectors. Like eyepins and headpins, I don't buy jump rings because I want to have a never-ending supply of the size, metal, color and shape that I need. Plus, they're so easy to make, as you will see below. For sturdy jump rings, I recommend using 18- or 20-gauge wire.

HELPFUL HINTS

For larger jump rings, coil the wire around a knitting needle or wooden dowel.

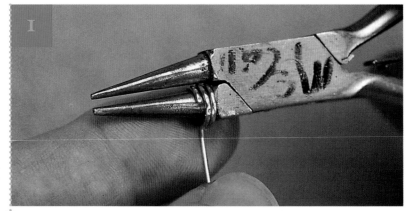

▼ Cut a length of wire and wrap one end around the tips of the round-nose pliers. Make sure the excess wire, called the feed line, is always on the widest part of the tips. Try to wrap the wire on the same part of the pliers so that you will have a coil that is a consistent size. Where you start the wire coil depends on the size rings you want to make.

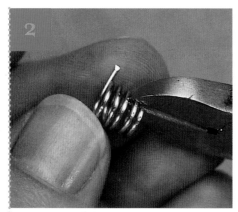

▼ Remove the wire coil from the pliers. To make single jump rings, clip down the middle of the coil with wire cutters. These cutters produce flat cuts on both ends of the wire so that you will have a cleaner closure. To make split jump rings, cut every other coil.

▼ Re-close the individual jump rings with your fingers or pliers if necessary.

HELPFUL HINTS

If your project requires only a few jump rings, you may find it easier to keep the coil handy and snip off jump rings as you need them.

MAKING OVAL JUMP RINGS

Jump rings don't necessarily have to be perfect circles. Some jewelry pieces look better and are more functional with oval jump rings. To start, refer to the directions on page 18 to make a round jump ring.

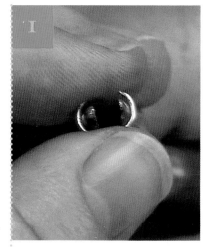

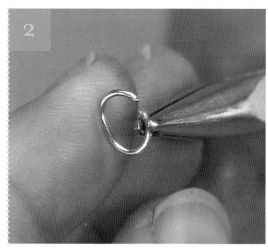

▼ Hold the round jump ring between your thumb and forefinger. Close the chain-nose pliers and insert the tips into the jump ring. Release the pliers and allow them to spring open.

▼ Grasp one end of the jump ring with your pliers and pull it into an oval while shaping with your fingers. Position the opening of the jump ring on the long side of the oval. That way, the stress point will be on each end of the oval and not on the opening itself.

▼ To make the jump ring stronger and less likely to pull apart, place it on a chasing block and pound it flat with a chasing hammer.

OPENING AND CLOSING JUMP RINGS

When opening and closing a jump ring, it is important to do so without distorting the shape. The best way to do this is to grip the ring tightly on each side of the opening with pliers. I recommend using two pairs of pliers for this, but in a pinch, you can grasp one side of the ring with your finger and thumb and the other side with pliers, as shown below.

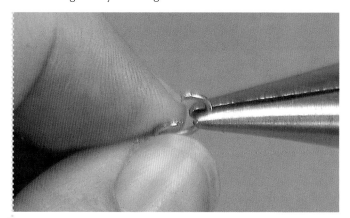

▼ **Open and Close with Pliers** – Grasp one side of the jump ring between your finger and thumb and the other side with chain-nose pliers. Twist your fingers and the pliers in opposite directions.

MAKING S-CLASPS

S-clasps are great for connecting clasps to close necklaces and bracelets. As the name describes, they are shaped like the letter *S*, which makes them as decorative as they are useful. For sturdy S-clasps, use 16-, 18- or 20-gauge wire. In the demonstration below, I am using 18-gauge wire. For a more polished look, it is a good idea to file the ends of the wire with a metal file before shaping it.

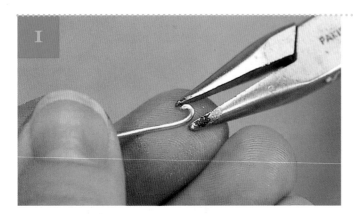

Cut a length of wire to 2½" (6.4cm) or the desired size for your clasp. Make a tiny loop on one end of the wire with round-nose pliers, then smash the loop with chain-nose pliers, as shown.

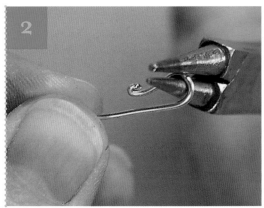

Bend the wire 180° in the opposite direction from the loop with the mid-section of your round-nose pliers to make the first part of the S-clasp.

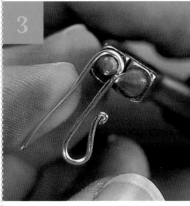

Move down about 1" (2.5cm) from the first curve and bend the wire 180° in the other direction.

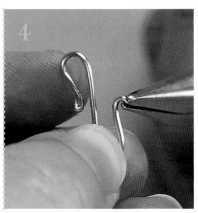

Repeat step 1 with the other end of the wire, going in the opposite direction from the second curve.

Place the S-clasp on a chasing block and pound it with a chasing hammer to flatten it.

USING CLAMSHELLS

Clamshells are used to connect single or multistrand beading wires together. I like to use them because they are inexpensive, easy to use and readily available in just about any metal. Clamshells come with connector loops that are either open, like hooks, or closed. I prefer using clamshells with open loop connectors (demonstrated below) because they are easy to connect to jump rings or clasps.

▼ Cut a piece of nylon beading cord to the desired length and add a dab of superglue to each end. Twist the cord to form a little "needle." Stick the needle through the hole in the middle of the open clamshell.

▼ Thread a tiny bead onto the cord and tie a square knot at the end of the cord. (For instructions, see page 16.) This stopper bead will keep the cord from slipping through the clamshell. Secure the knot with more superglue and trim excess cord.

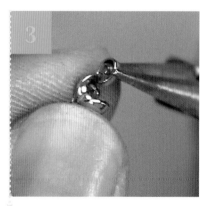

▼ Using round-nose pliers, bend the open connector loop on the clamshell down into the clam. This will make a sturdy connector when the clamshell is closed.

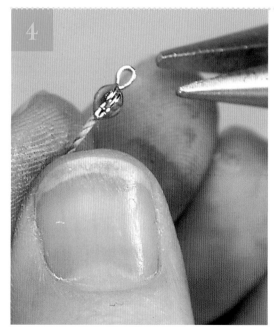

► Squeeze the clamshell shut with chain-nose pliers. Fasten a jump ring or clasp to the loop as desired. If you're using a soldered or split jump ring, attach the jump ring to the clamshell connector before closing it.

Get A Glue

Years ago, when manufacturers came out with colored and glittery glue sticks, I discovered that hot glue can be used for so much more than gluing objects together. I began using them to make faux wax seals for letters. The cool thing about the hot glue seals was they didn't break in the mail like regular wax seals. Since then, I've been putting hot glue on just about anything that doesn't move, as you'll discover from the projects in this chapter. I love showing the pieces to people and saying, "I'll betcha can't tell what this is made of." They are always surprised to learn that the designs are made by stamping into hot glue.

In addition to learning how to stamp into hot glue, this chapter will also teach you how to make a bead dangle. This is an easy process that will be used throughout the book. Use more or less wire for longer or shorter dangles, and vary the beads according to your personal taste. Remember, the sky is the limit when it comes to your creativity, and these projects are only the beginning of what you may come up with on your own!

SUNNY SIDE UP

This sun stamp has been one of my favorites from the moment I first drew him for Stamp Oasis. He is simple of line and bold in style, making him an excellent candidate for a hot glue pin. You can make this pin large enough to accommodate the entire sun image, or you can cut the foam core smaller so that the image is cropped and the rays go over the edge of the pin. I also think that it would be adorable to hang something other than another foam core piece from the bottom of the hinge, like a tiny handmade booklet of secrets, a locket or a timepiece. Wouldn't this make a cool watch pendant?

▼ Use a craft knife to cut a piece of foam core into a free-form shape slightly smaller than the sun rubber stamp. Cut a second foam core shape slightly smaller than the decorative rubber stamp. This will dangle off the first shape.

▼ Coat your stamps with clear embossing ink, pressing down hard to get as much ink as possible between the crevices. The ink works as a necessary release agent to ensure that the stamp and glue do not stick together.

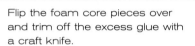

Apply a few lines of hot glue to the larger foam core shape. If the glue starts to dry, use your heat embossing tool to remelt it.

Impress the stamp into the glue with even pressure. Be careful not to press so hard that glue spills over the edges of the stamp. Hold the stamp in place until the glue is opaque, or cloudy, rather than crystal clear. To release, hold the rubber stamp with one hand, grasp the foam core piece in the other hand and pry them apart gently. Repeat with the smaller foam core piece and decorative stamp.

Flip the foam core pieces over and trim off the excess glue with a craft knife.

HELPFUL HINT

If you get a bad impression, just reheat the glue with your heat embossing tool and you're ready to go again.

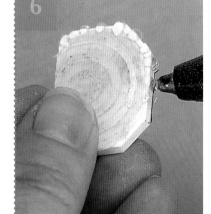

Apply decorative beads of hot glue to the sides of both pieces of foam core, covering all but the bottom edge of the large piece and the top edge of the small piece. This is where the hinge will be inserted.

Paint the front and sides of both pieces with dark green acrylic paint.

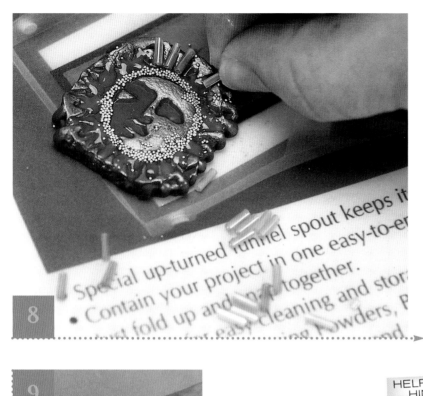

8

Mix gold and peridot acrylic paints, then use a dry paintbrush to paint small amounts onto the raised areas on both pieces of foam core. Allow the paint to dry completely. Apply Diamond Glaze to the pieces where you want the tiny gold beads to go. Sprinkle the beads over the wet Diamond Glaze, wait about ten minutes for the glaze to dry, then turn the pieces upside down and tap off the loose beads. Brush away any remaining loose beads with a dry paintbrush. Apply more Diamond Glaze and add green bugle beads as desired.

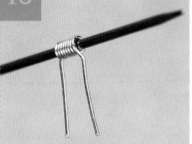

HELPFUL HINT

To avoid making a mess when working with tiny beads, I recommend using a bead tray like JudiKins's Snappy Tray.

Use wire cutters to cut a 4½" (11.4cm) piece of 20-gauge wire. Hold the wire against a knitting needle with your finger on the wire and the wire extending about 1" (2.5cm), as shown. This 1" (2.5cm) leg will remain straight as the rest of the wire is coiled around the knitting needle.

Wrap the remaining wire around the knitting needle until you have another 1" (2.5cm) leg remaining. Use chain-nose pliers to bend both legs so that they are aligned at the same angle.

Remove the wire coil from the knitting needle. Apply Gem-Tac to the bottom edge of the larger foam core piece and insert the legs of the coil into the foam, pushing until the coil rests against the foam. Set the piece aside to dry.

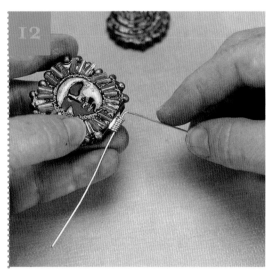

Cut a 3" (7.6cm) piece of 20-gauge wire. Use chain-nose pliers to bend one end of the wire at a right angle about 1¾" (4.5cm) from the end. String the wire through the coil at the bottom of the larger foam core piece until the angle meets the edge of the coil, as shown.

Bend the other side of the wire down so that both legs are parallel. Trim the legs to equal length if necessary.

Insert the legs protruding from the bottom of the larger piece through the channels.

Use a poultry lacing skewer to drill two holes, or channels, through the small foam core piece from top to bottom.

▼ Wrap the excess wire from the legs around the tips of your round-nose pliers to make decorative coils.

▼ To make the back of the pin, cut out two pieces of faux suede (or the material of your choice) slightly smaller than the pieces you will be covering. Flip the pin over and color the edges with a black permanent marker so that no white foam core will show after the backing is attached.

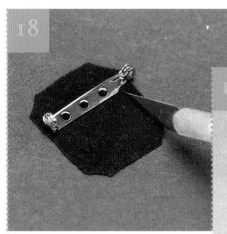

▼ Place a pinback over the larger piece of faux suede and cut slits in each end with a craft knife.

▼ Open the pinback and slip the ends through the slits in the faux suede. Use Gem-Tac to glue the large faux suede piece and pinback to the large foam core piece and the small faux suede piece to the small piece.

Try This!

While the stamped part of this piece is done the same way, the wire hanger at the bottom gives it a completely different look. To make it, wrap a wire coil around a dowel, then smash the coil flat and pull apart the loops.

TROPICAL TEASE

This little pin is a snap to make, and the Snappy Tray from JudiKins is great for controlling those tiny, travelling glass beads. Highlights are made with a gold leafing pen, and the outside edges are covered with tiny turquoise beads. The image, by Black Cat Designs, is special to me because I got it when I taught classes at an excellent convention in Australia. Since the piece is flat, this same design can be used to decorate cards and box tops. If you want to do something like this for your scrapbook, substitute a piece of cardstock for the foam core and follow the rest of the steps.

▶ Cut a piece of foam core to 1¾" x 1⅛" (3.2cm x 2.9cm) or slightly larger than the stamp you are using. Ink the stamp with clear embossing ink, apply hot glue to the foam core and stamp into the hot glue. Allow to cool, then remove the stamp. Use a craft knife to cut away the excess glue and foam core around the stamped image.

▼ Paint the front, back and sides of the piece with various colors of acrylic paint. Allow the paint to dry, then apply a coat of Diamond Glaze to the front and sides of the piece. Dip the sides into the tiny turquoise beads and allow the piece to dry. Tap off any excess beads.

▶ Highlight the raised portions of the stamped image with a gold leafing pen.

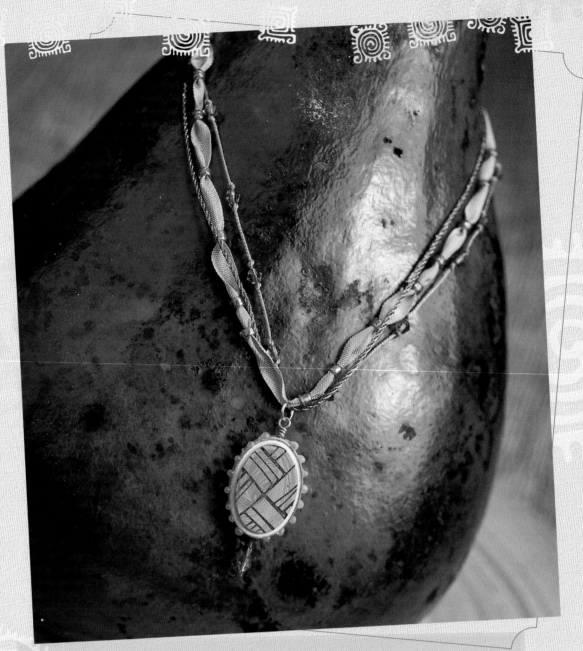

STYLE STONE SERENADE

Style Stones, by Clearsnap, are predrilled cultured stones that can be stamped, colored, painted and, as in this project, glued! They are really easy to use and fun to play with. You can find them in most rubber stamp stores, and they come in lots of great shapes and sizes. Experiment with a variety of inks on these stones. You may need to use your heat embossing tool to set, or dry, the ink, and you may need to use a cloth to work the ink onto the stone. Also try Clearsnap's Mica Magic inks to coat and stamp images onto the stones. The shimmery colors work beautifully in jewelry making and are permanent once dry.

MATERIALS

Decorative
rubber stamps
(JUDIKINS)

Style Stone (CLEARSNAP)

Crimp tubes

Decorative beads

Lobster claw clasp

Oval jump rings
(see page 19)

Brown nylon cord

Green nylon cord

Thin green
silk ribbon

22-gauge wire

Purple solvent ink

Green chalk ink

Scissors

Wire cutters

Chain-nose,
crimping and
round-nose pliers

Poultry lacing skewer

Fabri-Tac

Hot glue gun and
glue sticks

Heat embossing tool

 To color the Style Stone, push it into the chalk ink, then rub the ink around the stone with your finger. Allow the ink to dry.

HELPFUL HINT

To dry ink
or paint
quickly,
heat it with
a heat
embossing
tool.

Ink the decorative stamp with purple solvent ink, then stamp onto the stone. Allow the ink to dry.

Apply decorative beads of hot glue around the edges of the stone, making sure not to cover the holes at the top and bottom of the stone where the jewelry connectors will go.

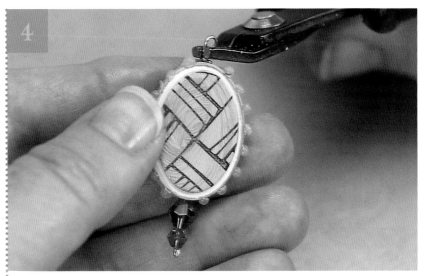

To make a bead dangle, start by forming a headpin by cutting a 5" (13cm) length of wire (for this project, I used 22-gauge wire) and flattening one end with crimping pliers. String a few decorative beads and the stone onto the headpin. Make a loop at the top of the wire with round-nose pliers, then twist the wire around the neck of the headpin a couple of times. Use wire cutters to cut off the excess wire, then use crimping pliers to tuck the end of the wire flat against the wrapped neck of the headpin.

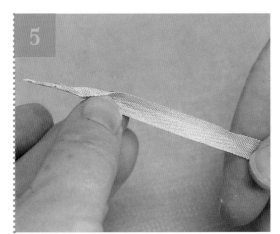

Cut the green ribbon and the green and brown cords to 21" (53.3cm) or the desired length for your pendant. Apply Fabri-Tac to one end of the ribbon, fold it a few times and pinch it into a tiny point.

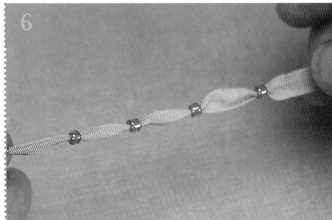

Thread beads onto the ribbon, spacing them evenly, as shown.

Thread a smaller decorative bead onto the green cord. Tie a knot and stick the poultry lacing skewer into the knot before pulling it taut. Pull the skewer toward the bead, then tighten the knot. Repeat this step to tie several more beads onto the cord, spacing them about 1" (2.5cm) apart.

Bundle the beaded ribbon, beaded green cord and plain brown cord together and thread them through a crimp tube. Crimp the tube closed with crimping pliers, as shown on page 16. Attach an oval jump ring to the end of the crimp tube, then attach one end of the lobster claw clasp to the jump ring. Repeat with the other end of the necklace.

Open an oval jump ring and thread the ribbon and cords at the center of the necklace through the opening. Attach the dangle from step 4, then close the jump ring.

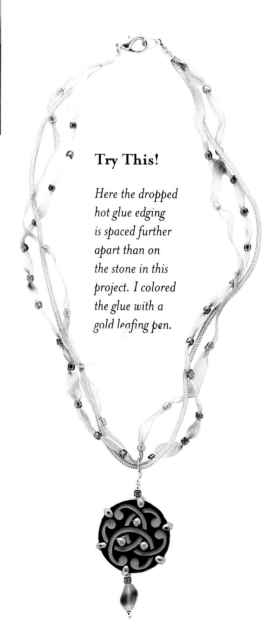

Try This!

Here the dropped hot glue edging is spaced further apart than on the stone in this project. I colored the glue with a gold leafing pen.

WHO'S IN MY HOUSE?

This Rubber Moon stamp is another image that speaks to me. On some days, I feel like I am running back and forth in indecision. On other days, I feel like I am the master of my house, and I love it! You could make your pin or pendant the size of the image itself, or you could make it even larger and add more beads and swirls of hot glue. It would also look cool if you wrapped and twisted beaded wire around the perimeter of the foam core piece. There are lots of possibilities, so go ahead and experiment.

MATERIALS

House rubber stamp
(RUBBER MOON)

Foam core board

Assorted decorative
beads for dangles

Tiny gold beads

Bead tray

Black nylon cord

20-gauge wire

Clear embossing ink

Gold, silver
and metallic red
acrylic paints

Paintbrush

Craft knife

Wire cutters

Chain-nose pliers,
crimping and
round-nose pliers

½" (1.3cm)
wooden dowel

Knitting needle

Diamond Glaze

Gem-Tac

Superglue

Hot glue gun and
glue sticks

Use a craft knife to cut out a foam core house shape slightly larger than the house on the stamp.

Ink the stamp with clear embossing ink. Apply hot glue to the middle of the foam core piece and impress the stamp into the glue. Allow it to cool, then remove the stamp.

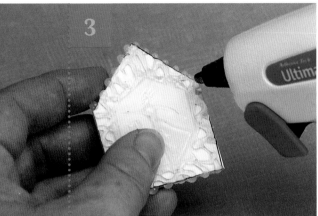

▼ Make a decorative border around the unstamped areas of the foam core piece with hot glue. Allow the glue to cool.

▼ Paint the stamped area of the glue with metallic red acrylic paint and the decorative border with gold acrylic paint. Drybrush a light topcoat of silver acrylic paint over the raised areas.

▼ Apply Diamond Glaze to the entire piece and sprinkle it with tiny gold beads. Allow the Diamond Glaze to dry, then tap off any loose beads.

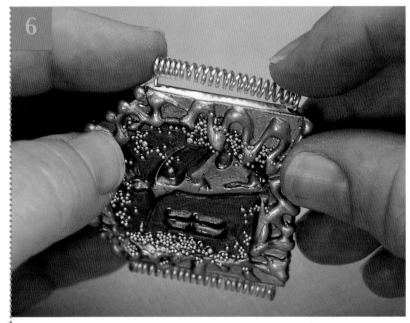

▼ Use wire cutters to cut two 10" (2.5cm) pieces of 20-gauge wire. Wrap one of the wires around a knitting needle to form a coil, leaving 1" (2.5cm) legs on each end. Remove the wire from the knitting needle and pull the coil apart slightly. Repeat with the other wire. Apply Gem-Tac along the left and right sides of the foam core piece and stick the legs of the wires into the piece.

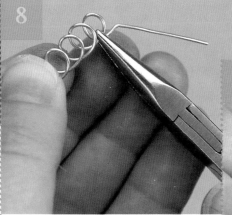

Cut a 7" (1.8cm) piece of 20-gauge wire and wrap it around a ½" (1.3cm) dowel five times, leaving equal legs on each end. Use chain-nose pliers to bend the legs so that they are parallel. Slide the coil off the dowel and flatten it to one side with your fingers as shown.

Grasp one end of the coil with chain-nose pliers and the other end with your fingers. Pull outward to separate the loops. Rebend the legs if necessary.

Apply Gem-Tac to the bottom of the foam core piece. Stick the legs into the foam, pushing until the loops meet the bottom of the foam. Allow the glue to dry.

Cut a piece of black nylon cord to the desired length of your pendant and thread the ends of the cord through the side coils. Tie knots at each end, trim off the excess and secure with a dab of superglue. Make several bead dangles with 20-gauge wire and decorative beads as described on page 34, step 4, stringing the headpin wires through the loops to attach them to the necklace before wrapping the excess wire around the top of the pin.

CALYPSO QUEEN

This project is interesting because the second coiled channel was actually a problem solver. You see, I didn't make the first coil large enough to hold three strands of beads, so I came up with this creative solution. Don't let little mistakes like this bother you. Instead, turn them into unique design elements! I'm particularly fond of the rubber stamp used in this project because of the clean lines and fun, curly design. The multiple layers of metallic paint and matching beads make it a colorful, yet sophisticated, necklace.

MATERIALS

Decorative
rubber stamps
(JudiKins)

Foam core board

Faux suede

Black, gold and
turquoise seed beads

Crimp beads

Cylindrical glass bead

Tiny gold beads

Bead tray

Two jewelry cones

.015 beading wire

18-gauge wire

20-gauge wire

Clear embossing ink

Black and metallic
acrylic paints

Black permanent
marker

Paintbrush

Craft knife

Wire cutters

Chain-nose,
crimping and
round-nose pliers

Chasing block and
hammer

Knitting needle

Poultry lacing skewer

Diamond Glaze

Gem-Tac

Hot glue gun and
glue sticks

Cut a piece of foam core to the size of your stamp. Ink the stamp with clear embossing ink. Apply hot glue to the foam core piece and stamp the image into the hot glue. Allow the glue to cool, then remove the stamp. Trim away the excess glue from the edges with a craft knife.

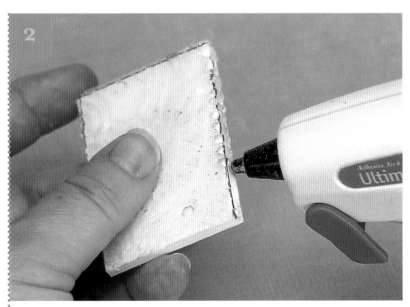

Apply decorative beads of hot glue around the bottom and sides of the foam core piece along the edges. Don't worry about the pen lines; you will paint over them.

Paint the stamped image with black acrylic paint, then drybrush it with a topcoat of various metallic paints. Allow the paint to dry completely.

Apply Diamond Glaze to the piece and sprinkle tiny gold beads over the wet glaze. Allow to dry, then flip the piece over and tap off any loose beads. Add more highlights of Diamond Glaze if desired.

Cut a 10" (2.5cm) piece of 20-gauge wire and wrap it around a knitting needle, leaving 1" (2.5cm) legs on both ends. Pull the coil apart when it is still on the knitting needle. Use chain-nose pliers to bend the legs so that they are parallel, then remove the coil from the needle.

Apply Gem-Tac to the top edge of the foam core piece and push the legs of the wire coil all the way into the foam.

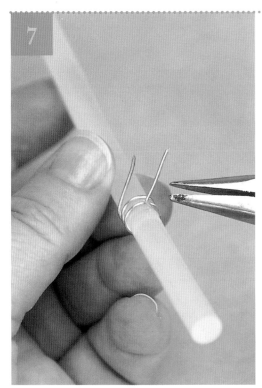

> Cut a 4" (10cm) piece of 20-gauge wire and wrap it around a glue stick, marker or another larger cylinder, leaving equal legs on each end. Use chain-nose pliers to bend the legs so that they are parallel.

Flip the foam core piece over and color the edges with black permanent marker. Bend the legs of the larger coil from step 7 outward and glue them to the back of the foam core piece with Gem-Tac.

Cut a piece of faux suede (or the material of your choice) slightly smaller than the foam core piece and glue it to the back. Set the piece aside for use in step 14.

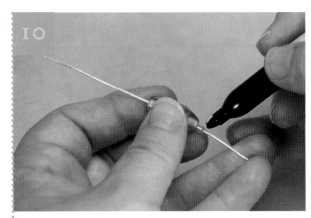

Cut a piece of 20-gauge wire to about 5" (12.7cm). Place a cylindrical glass bead in the center of the wire and mark the approximate spot where the bead ends. (The bead does not look centered in this photo because some of the wire is under my finger.)

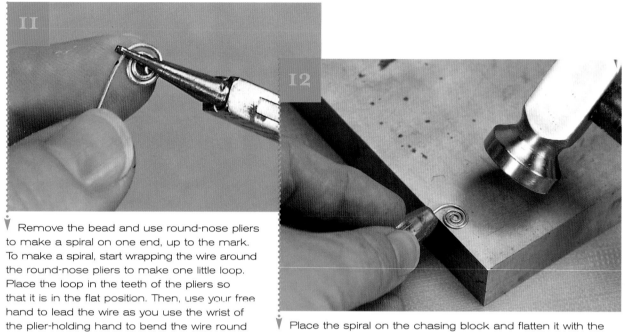

Remove the bead and use round-nose pliers to make a spiral on one end, up to the mark. To make a spiral, start wrapping the wire around the round-nose pliers to make one little loop. Place the loop in the teeth of the pliers so that it is in the flat position. Then, use your free hand to lead the wire as you use the wrist of the plier-holding hand to bend the wire round and round until you come to a spiral size that you like.

Place the spiral on the chasing block and flatten it with the chasing hammer. Slip the long bead back on the wire. Spiral and flatten the other end. Bend the spirals down so that they curl under the bead.

Cut a 4" (10.2cm) piece of 20-gauge wire and slip it through the wired bead, as shown. Center the wire and bend the legs in the opposite direction of the spirals.

Use a poultry lacing skewer to drill diagonal channels from the bottom edges to the side edges of the foam core body of the pendant.

▼ Feed the legs of the wired bead into the channels, then coil the excess wires decoratively with round-nose pliers.

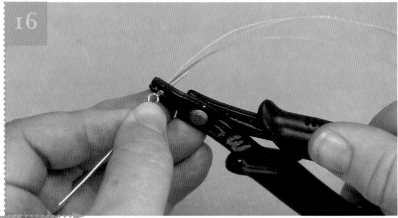

Cut a 2" (5.1cm) piece of 18-gauge wire and make an eyepin on one end, as described on page 17. Squeeze the eye loop slightly with chain-nose pliers to make it into an oval. Cut three 32" (81.3cm) pieces of beading wire and thread all three wires through a crimp bead, through the eyepin, then back through the crimp bead. Crimp the bead with crimping pliers. Clip the tail ends of the wires about ¹⁄₁₆" (1.5mm) from the crimp bead.

▼ Slide the straight part of the eyepin through one end of the cone-shaped jewelry finding and make another eye loop on the other end with round-nose pliers.

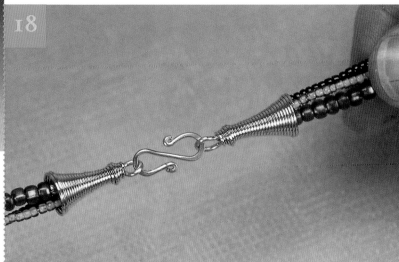

▼ Thread seed beads onto the beading wires as desired, then repeat steps 16 and 17 to fasten the other cone-shaped finding to the other end of the necklace. Make an S-clasp (see page 20), and attach it to the eye on each cone to fasten.

Fabric Favorites

In this chapter, you will discover how easy it is to transform solid fabric and undecorated buttons into beautiful stamped jewelry. Stamping on fabric with ink or paint is one of my favorite things to do. The fabric I prefer to use is muslin because it is sturdy, durable and holds color well. I usually decorate large pieces of muslin, about 18" x 18" (46cm x 46cm), at a time. This gives me enough fabric to make lots of different projects, including little purses, bags and sculptural jewelry. Rarely do I paint a piece as I am making a project. Rather, I spend a block of time concentrating on making different designs on one large piece of fabric.

In addition to the beautiful fabric used to decorate the jewelry in this chapter, I have also incorporated button blanks, which are simply buttons that have blank spaces where jewels would normally be. They are incredibly inexpensive, and the blank spaces are the perfect place to glue tiny stamped images. I found my button blanks in the garment district in Los Angeles, but you can also use flat-topped buttons from your local fabric store.

COTTON CONTESSA

Funky-cool but still kind of elegant in spite of its humble beginnings, this necklace is a real conversation starter. The "beads" are actually clear plastic tubes covered in stamped fabric. The plastic tubes can be found in hardware or electrical supply stores. Just be sure to buy the kind that you can easily cut with scissors. The glimmer of the delicas definitely catches people's eyes, and they will want to look closer to see just how you made this necklace. It also features a clamshell, which is a finding that closes up like a clam, usually over a knot tied over a stopper bead.

MATERIALS

Decorative
rubber stamps
(JudiKins)

Plastic tubing

18"x 18"
(46cm x 46cm)
piece of muslin

Delicas

E beads

Leaf beads

Silver spacer beads

Stopper bead

Clamshells

Purchased clasp

Extender chain

Nylon beading cord

20- and 22-gauge
wires

Acrylic paints
in various colors

Foam brushes

Scissors

Wire cutters

Chain-nose,
crimping and
round-nose pliers

Fabri-Tac

Superglue

Heat embossing tool

Paper plate

Water in small bowl

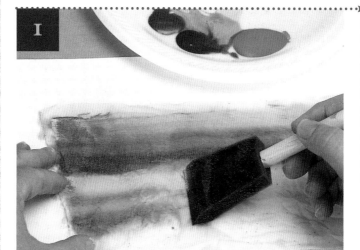

1 Wet the muslin by dunking it in water and wringing it out. Squeeze small amounts of acrylic paints onto a paper plate. (For this project, I used red, yellow, green and purple.) Dip a foam brush into the small bowl of water, then into the paint, and drag it over the muslin. Dry the muslin with a heat embossing tool, moving the tool around so you don't burn the muslin or your hands.

HELPFUL HINT

It is important to tap the paint onto the stamp rather than brush it on. The brushing motion will only get paint into the grooves of the stamp and, at the same time, brush it off the top of the stamp.

2 Tap a dry foam brush into the acrylic paint, then tap the brush onto the rubber stamp. Tap the stamp onto the muslin; the tapping motion will lightly impress the image into the fabric. Continue stamping in layers and in different colors. Dry the paint with the heat embossing tool.

HELPFUL HINT

If you press the stamp onto the fabric with firm pressure as you would with paper, the paint will goosh (yes, that's a technical term!) out from under the stamp and leave a bad impression.

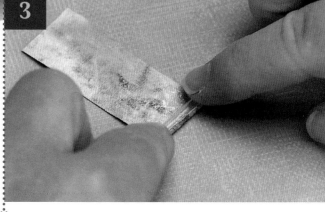

3 Cut nine plastic tubes to sizes varying from ½" to 2" (1.3cm to 5.1cm). Place the longest tube on your work surface and arrange the shorter tubes on each side. Cut a 2" (5.1cm) strip of muslin, then apply Fabri-Tac to the plain side of the muslin strip and wrap it around the plastic tube to make a tube bead. Repeat with the muslin to cover the remaining tubes. Set the excess decorated muslin aside for use in other projects.

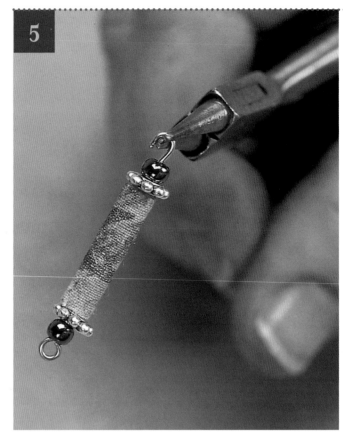

▼ Use wire cutters to cut twenty-two 1¼" (3.2cm) pieces of 20-gauge wire. Make nine of the wires into eyepins. Make the remaining thirteen wires into headpins.

► To make the tube bead dangles, string each eyepin with one E bead, one spacer bead, one fabric tube bead, one spacer bead and one E bead, then loop the end of the wire into an eye and wrap the remaining wire around the neck of the dangle.

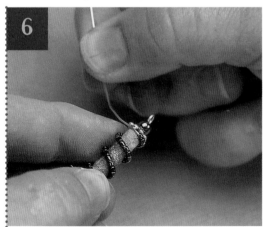

▼ Cut nine 7" (17.8cm) pieces of 22-gauge wire. Wrap a piece of wire around the neck of a tube bead dangle between the top spacer bead and the tube bead. String delicas onto the wire, then coil it around the tube bead. Wrap the end of the wire around the bottom of the dangle between the tube bead and the bottom spacer bead. Trim the excess wire with wire cutters and tuck the end of the wire flat against the wrapped neck with crimping pliers. Repeat with the remaining wire and tube bead dangles, and set aside for use in step 9.

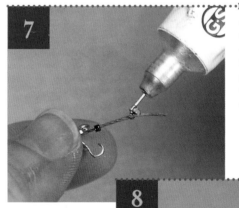

► Cut a 16" (40.6cm) piece of nylon beading cord and slip a clamshell onto one end of the cord. Thread a stopper bead onto the cord, then tie a knot and secure the knot with a dab of superglue. Snip off the excess cord.

► With the clamshell still open, use round-nose pliers to bend the open connector loop down into the clamshell. Pinch the clamshell closed with chain-nose pliers. (For more about clamshells, see page 21.)

This photo shows my bead stringing sequence in detail. Feel free to string the glass beads with the fabric tube beads in any order you like. To make the leaf dangles shown here, string the headpins with one delica, one E bead, one leaf bead, one E bead and one delica. Then loop the end of the wire into an eye and wrap the remaing wire around the neck.

Repeat the clamshell process from steps 7 and 8 on the other end of the cord. Cut a 2" (5.1cm) piece of extender chain and hold an end link from the chain with round- and chain-nose pliers. Twist the pliers in opposite directions to open the link. Fasten the link to one of the clamshell connector hooks and twist the link closed.

To make a pretty finish to the extender chain, thread delica and E beads onto a 2" (5cm) headpin. Make a loop at the end of the headpin and attach it to the chain.

Hold the looped wire with round-nose pliers in one hand and use the other hand to wrap the excess wire around the end of the charm with chain-nose pliers.

To finish the necklace, attach one end of a purchased clasp, such as the spring-loaded one shown here, to one clamshell connector hook and the other end of the clasp to the other clamshell connector hook with chain-nose pliers.

REGAL RAG

This is another piece that is fun to wear. From the grocery store to my stamping classes, people are always grabbing my wrist to have a closer look to see what it is. This is one of the easiest bracelets that I know how to make. The design calls for so few beads that it is a great way to use up those odds and ends you have left over after a larger beading project. The basis for this design is a ladder stitch, which aptly describes the beading process. You can see how varying the length or width of the fabric-covered "rungs" and changing the size or number of the beads on the "rails" will change the look of the overall project.

MATERIALS

Decorative rubber stamps
(HERO ARTS)

Foam core board

Decorated muslin
(see page 49)

E beads

Seed beads

Glass and handmade decorative beads

Toggle clasp

Thin black-and-white checked ribbon

10 lb. fishing wire

18-gauge wire

Metal ruler

Craft knife

Scissors

Wire cutters

Chain-nose and round-nose pliers

Two No. 13 beading needles

Poultry lacing skewer

Fabri-Tac

Superglue

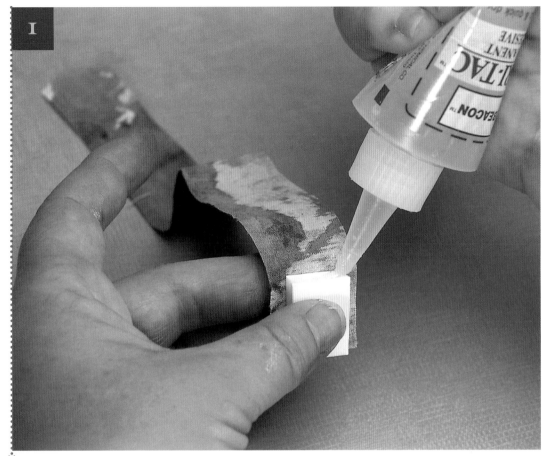

1 Cut the foam core board into three ⅝" x 1" (1.6cm x 2.5cm) pieces, then cut three 1⅛" (2.9) wide strips of decorated muslin. Use Fabri-Tac to wrap each foam core piece with a strip of decorated muslin.

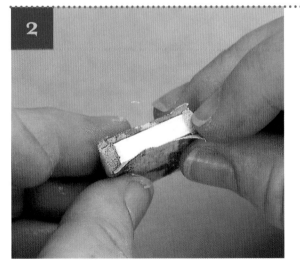

Trim off the edges of the muslin and fold in the sides, top and bottom.

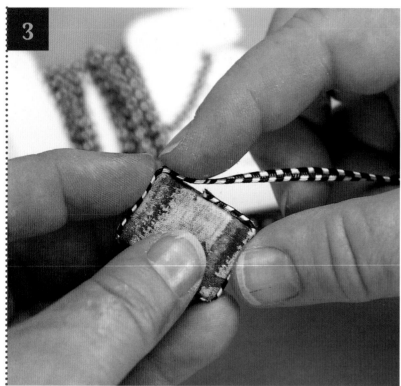

▼ Apply Fabri-Tac around the edges of the covered foam core pieces, then wrap with thin black-and-white checked ribbon. Trim off the excess ribbon.

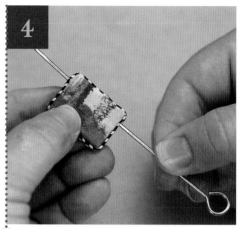

▼ Use a poultry lacing skewer to drill two channels in each foam core piece, ½" (1.3cm) in from each side, from top to bottom.

Cut six 2" (5.1cm) pieces of 18-gauge wire and feed one piece through each channel. Use round-nose pliers to make loops at both ends of each wire. Set the foam core pieces aside for use in step 14.

▼ Cut two more 2" (5.1cm) pieces of 18-gauge wire and make them into eyepins. String each eyepin with one E bead, one glass bead, one large handmade bead and two E beads. End each wire with another eye loop and set both bead dangles aside for use in step 15.

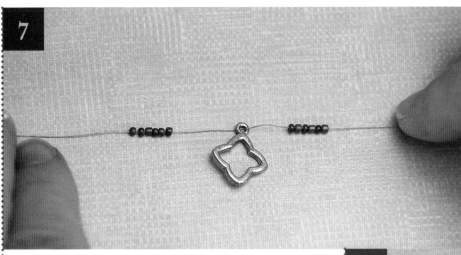

7

Cut a piece of fishing wire to five times the size of your wrist. Thread each end of the wire with No. 13 beading needles, leaving a 5" (14cm) tail on each end. String one end of the toggle clasp onto the wire and center it, then thread six seed beads onto each side (wire 1 and wire 2), alternating colors.

8

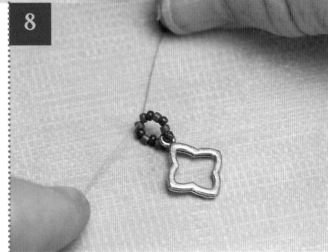

Tie a square knot to make a beaded circle.

9

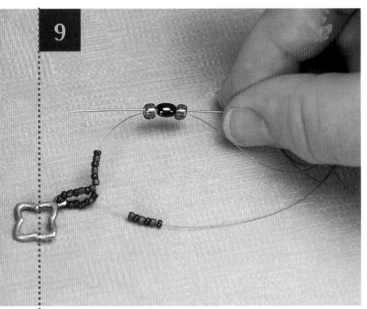

String wire 1 with six seed beads, one E bead, one oval bead and one E bead. String wire 2 with six seed beads, then thread it back through the E–oval–E series on wire 1. Pull the wires taut to make another beaded circle.

10

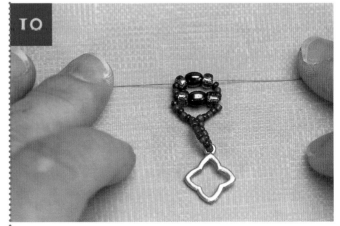

Repeat two more times to make a total of three beaded circles in this manner.

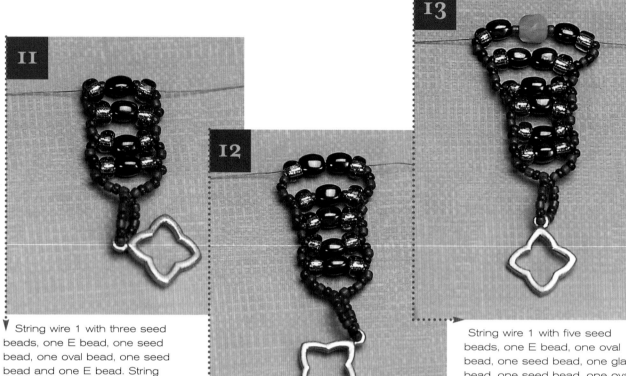

▼ String wire 1 with three seed beads, one E bead, one seed bead, one oval bead, one seed bead and one E bead. String wire 2 with three seed beads, then thread it through the E–seed–oval–seed–E series on wire 1.

▼ String wire 1 with four seed beads, one E bead, two oval beads and one E bead. String wire 2 with four seed beads, then thread it through the E–oval–oval–E series on wire 1.

String wire 1 with five seed beads, one E bead, one oval bead, one seed bead, one glass bead, one seed bead, one oval bead and one E bead. String wire 2 with five seed beads, then thread it through the E–oval– seed–glass–seed–oval–E series on wire 1.

▶ String wire 1 with six seed beads, then thread it through the first wire loop on one of the foam core pieces from step 5. Continue stringing wire 1 with one seed bead, one oval bead, one seed bead, then out through the other wire loop on the foam core piece. Repeat this sequence with wire 2.

15

String wire 1 with three seed beads, one oval bead, one bead dangle from step 6, one oval bead, three seed beads, one loop of another foam core piece, one seed bead, one oval bead, one seed bead, then out the other loop of the foam core piece. Repeat this sequence with wire 2.

16

Repeat steps 7–13 in reverse to finish the bracelet, as shown here.

17

End as you began, with six seed beads, the other end of the toggle clasp, six seed beads and a square knot. Secure the knot with a dot of superglue. Before you clip the ends off the wire, feed it back through a few of the seed beads to conceal the ends.

Try This!

This colorful piece is also made with two lengths of fishing wire. Notice the pretty, small beads strung to cross over the foam core pillow beads.

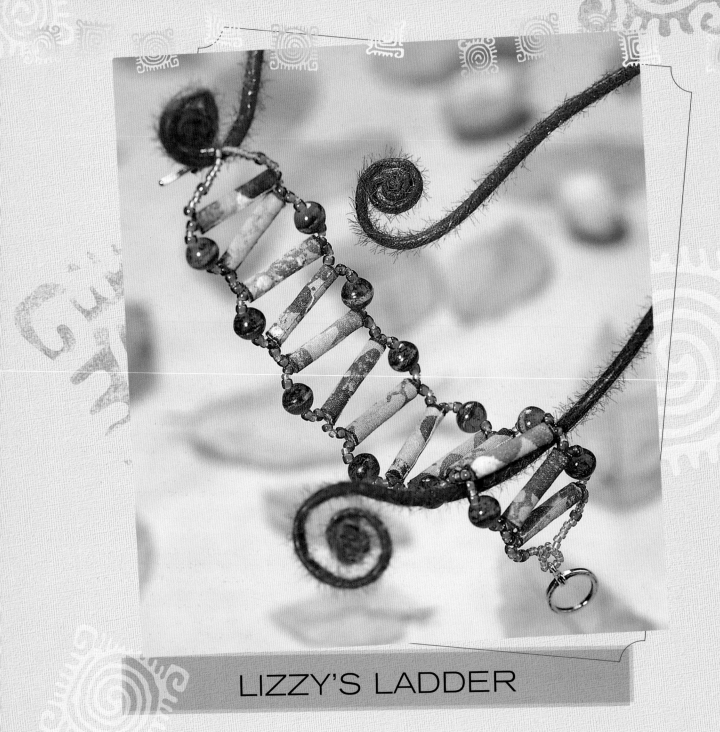

LIZZY'S LADDER

Okay, maybe I have been out here in the desert for too long, but to me, the colors in this project remind me of little lizards running up a ladder. Like the Regal Rag bracelet on page 52, this project is also based on a ladder stitch. The difference is that the rungs of this ladder are diagonal to each other instead of parallel. The construction technique is almost identical, except that the number of beads on the rails has been changed. If you add more beads to every other side and fewer to the rest of the rail, you can vary the degree of slant in the overall design. That goes for changing the bead sizes, as well. Try experimenting with this design by shortening the fabric-covered rungs of the ladder.

MATERIALS

Decorative
rubber stamps
(JudiKins)

Plastic tubing

Decorated muslin
(see page 49)

E beads

Large round beads

Seed beads

Toggle clasp

20 lb. monofilament
line

Purple permanent
marker

Scissors

Fabri-Tac

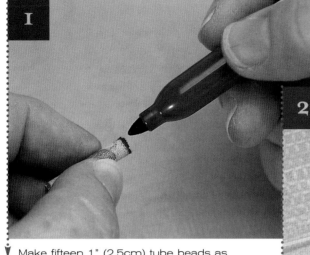

▼ Make fifteen 1" (2.5cm) tube beads as described on page 49, steps 1–3. Color the ends of the tube beads with purple permanent marker to add dimension.

▼ Cut a piece of monofilament wire to five times the size of your wrist. Center one end of the toggle clasp on the wire, then thread five seed beads onto each side of the clasp (wire 1 and wire 2). Tie a square knot, as described on page 16, to make a beaded circle.

▶ String wire 1 with six seed beads, one E bead, three seed beads, one E bead and one tube bead. Repeat on wire 2, omitting the tube bead. Thread wire 2 back through the tube bead on wire 1 and pull taut. Then, string wire 1 with one E bead, one seed bead, one large round bead, one E bead, one seed bead, one E bead and one tube bead. String wire 2 with one E bead, one seed bead and one E bead, then thread wire 2 back through the tube bead on wire 1. Repeat as desired, alternating long and short sequences on wires 1 and 2. To finish, repeat step 2 on the end of the wire with the other end of the toggle clasp.

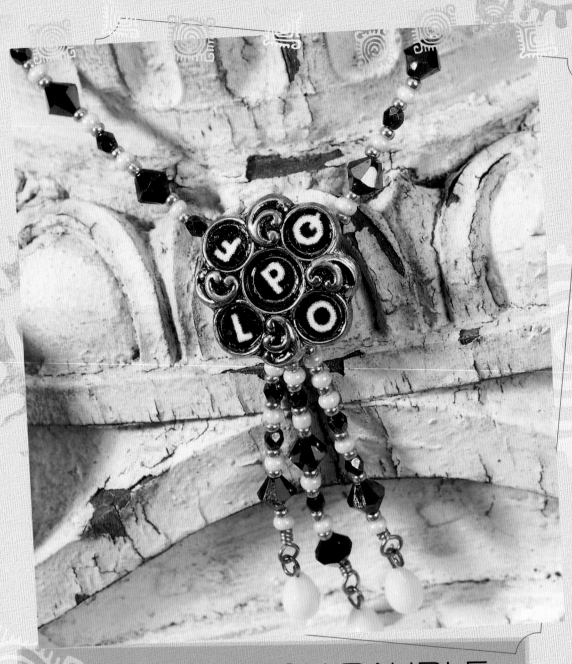

ALPHA BUTTON BAUBLE

You just can't have too many text and alphabet stamps! The letters in little black circles are perfect for this project. In one class, I had all my students busily cutting out tiny circles of stamped letters and images, when one of them said, "Why aren't we using a hole punch for this?" Why indeed! Since then, hole punches have made cutting out tiny images and letters a whole lot easier for me and my students! I use button blanks here, but any type of flat-faced button will work. Also, if you don't like the finish on a button, use permanent ink and markers to make it whatever color you like. Look for buttons with shanks on them so you will have something to string the cord through.

MATERIALS

Tiny alphabet
rubber stamps
(PSX)

White cardstock

Button blank with
several open spaces

Black faceted beads
in various sizes

Crimp beads

Gold seed beads

Ivory E beads

Ivory teardrop-
shaped beads

Lobster claw clasp

Extender chain

Beading wire

22-gauge wire

Black solvent ink

Paintbrush

¼" (0.6cm) hole
punch

Wire cutters

Chain-nose,
crimping and
round-nose pliers

Diamond Glaze

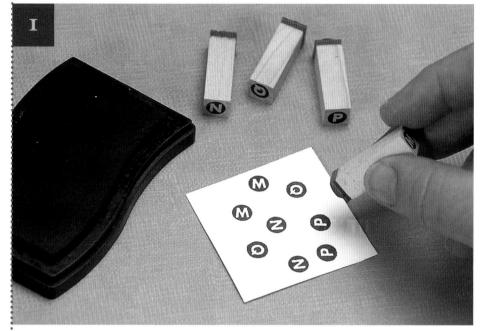

▼ Ink several letters from the tiny alphabet stamps with black solvent ink
and stamp them onto white cardstock.

▼ Punch out the letters with the hole punch and adhere
them to the spaces on the button blank with Diamond
Glaze. Apply a thin coat of Diamond Glaze to the paper
pieces and spread it around with your finger or a paintbrush
to seal.

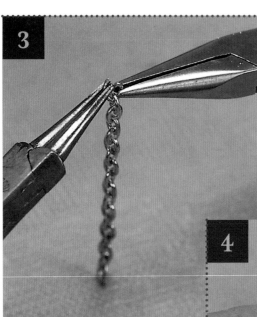

► Use wire cutters to cut two 2" (5.1cm) pieces of extender chain. Hold an end link from one of the chains with round-nose and chain-nose pliers, and twist the pliers in opposite directions to open the link.

▼ Make a split jump ring with a piece of 22-gauge wire, as described on page 18. Slip the split jump ring onto the open link of the chain, then reclose the link by twisting the pliers the other way. Attach a split jump ring to the other piece of extender chain in the same manner.

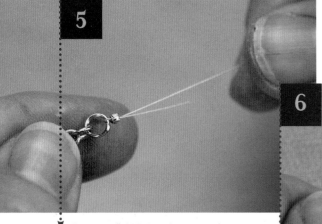

▼ Cut a 16" (40.6cm) piece of beading wire. Slide a crimp bead onto one end of the wire, loop the wire through one of the split jump rings, then back through the crimp bead. Crimp the crimp bead with crimping pliers.

▼ Thread the first 1" (2.5cm) of beading wire alternating seed and E beads, then continue threading seed, E and faceted black beads onto the wire for about 7" (17.8cm) or the desired hanging length for your button blank bauble. Thread the button blank from step 2 onto the wire through the button shank, then continue threading beads in the reverse order.

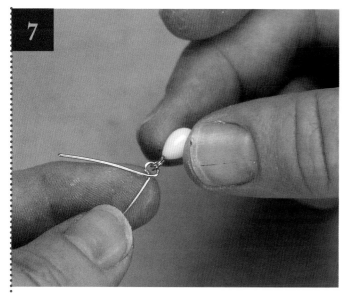

7 Cut a 3" (7.6cm) piece of 22-gauge wire and use round-nose pliers to make a loop near one end. Make a bead dangle using a teardrop bead. Slip the dangle onto the loop, then close the loop.

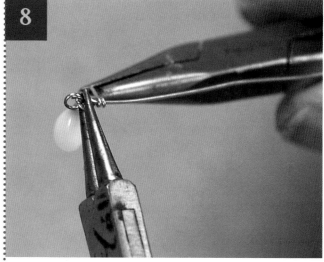

8 Hold the wire loop with round-nose pliers and grasp the short end of the wire with chain-nose pliers. Wrap the short end of the wire around the base of the loop two or three times, then trim off the excess. Feed various beads onto the remaining wire. Repeat to make two more dangles.

HELPFUL HINT

When you are stringing necklaces, consider using smaller beads at the back, closest to the clasps. This will make the necklace lie flatter underneath clothing, and it will feel less bulky along the back of your neck.

9 Attach all three dangles to the button shank. If the shank is too small, add a jump ring to the shank and fasten the dangles to the jump ring. The back of the necklace should look like this photograph.

10 To finish, connect split jump rings to both ends of the necklace as you did in step 4. Connect the lobster claw clasp to one split jump ring and attach it to the other split jump ring, as shown.

ALL BUTTONED UP

Designed to accommodate vintage photos and ephemera, stamped images, text and small found objects, this beaded bracelet is excellent for all types of crafters. Bead lovers will enjoy the prospect of using any number and color of different beads; stampers and papercrafters will love the embossing technique; and archivists will be excited to transform buttons, beads and stamped artwork into a wonderfully wearable memory bracelet. Once you get the rhythm going, this bracelet is very easy to construct. It is merely a series of repetitive loops crossing over one another, like a whole lot of figure eights strung together. Trust me, this one will be easy to make with not a needle in sight!

MATERIALS

Decorative
rubber stamps
(STAMPOTIQUE)

Black cardstock

Five button blanks

Imm beads

Chip beads

Crimp beads

E beads

Seed beads

Box clasp

Beading wire

White embossing ink
and powder

Black permanent
marker

Scissors

Wire cutters

Crimping pliers

Heat embossing tool

Diamond Glaze

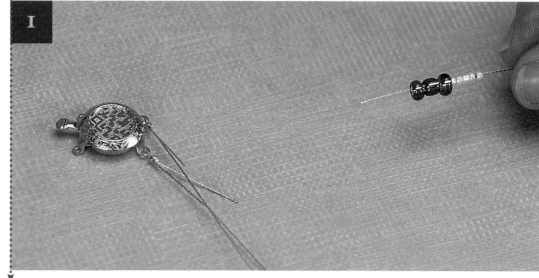

1

▼ Cut two pieces of beading wire (wire 1 and wire 2) to five times the size of your wrist. Attach both wires to one end of the clasp with crimp beads. Thread five seed beads and three E beads onto wire 1.

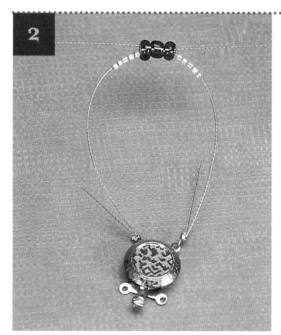

2

▶ String five seed beads onto wire 2, then thread it through the three E bead connector series on wire 1 and pull taut to make a loop.

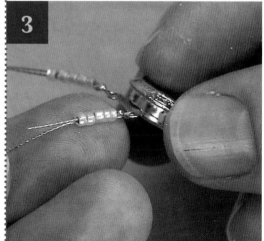

3

▼ Thread the wire ends from step 1 through the five seed beads on each side to conceal the ends.

▼ String wire 1 with eleven seed beads, one E bead, one button and one E bead. String wire 2 with eleven seed beads, then thread it through the E-button-E sequence on wire 1 and pull taut.

▼ String wire 1 with eleven seed beads and three E beads. String wire 2 with eleven seed beads, then thread it through the E beads on wire 1.

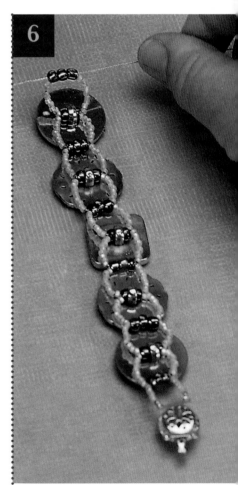

▼ Repeat steps 4 and 5 with the remaining buttons.

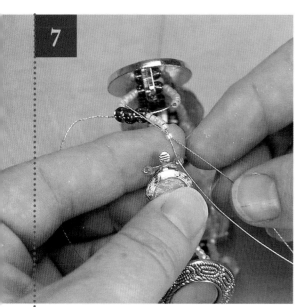

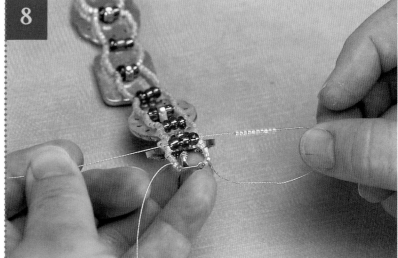

String wire 1 with six seed beads, then thread it through the other end of the clasp, back through the sixth seed bead and pull taut. Repeat this step with wire 2. Lay the bracelet out flat.

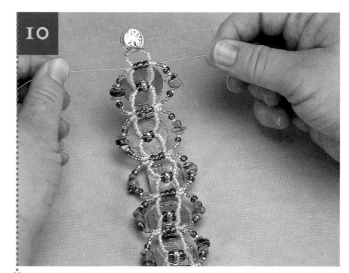

String wire 1 with ten seed beads, then thread it back through the first three E bead connector series you made in step 2. Repeat on wire 2, threading it through the E bead connector series the other way.

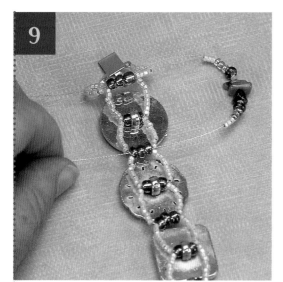

String wire 1 with three seed beads, three 1mm beads, one E bead, one seed bead and three chip beads, then repeat in reverse order. (You may need to adjust the beading sequence in this step, depending on the size of your buttons.) Pass the wire through the next three E bead connector series so that it goes around the button. Repeat the entire sequence on wire 2.

Repeat step 9 all the way to the end, essentially making a beaded loop around every button.

▶ To make an end loop, string wire 1 with ten seed beads and one crimp bead, then thread the wire through the clasp and back down through the crimp bead again.

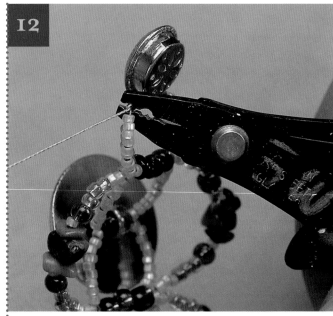

▼ Pull taut and crimp as described on page 16. Repeat with wire 2. Conceal the excess wire by tucking it into a few of the seed beads near the clasp.

▶ Ink the decorative stamp with embossing ink and stamp onto black cardstock. Sprinkle the wet ink with embossing powder. Tap the excess powder off the image and return it to the container. Heat with a heat embossing tool to melt the powder and create a raised image on the cardstock.

14 Color inside the button blanks with a black permanent marker.

15 Cut out pieces from the embossed cardstock to the size of the button blanks and glue them in place with Diamond Glaze. Don't worry if your shapes aren't exact. The black permanent marker will mask any irregular cuts.

16 To finish, apply Diamond Glaze over the buttons and spread it around with your finger to smooth out any bubbles.

Poly Playthings

This section encompasses two of my favorite polymer playthings: polymer clay and polymer plastic in the form of shrink plastic. Polymer clay is a pliable, bendable compound that can be molded, shaped, sculpted and baked into a hardened piece. It comes in every color imaginable, and even in liquid form. There are several brands on the market, including Sculpey, FIMO, and my brands of choice, Premo! and Kato Polyclay. Polymer clay must be warmed and kneaded with your hands, or conditioned, until it is soft enough to mold. Hand-conditioned clay can be rolled through a pasta machine for further conditioning and to make sheets of clay in varying thicknesses. Once a piece is sculpted, it must be baked in the oven to harden.

Shrink plastic is thin, flexible plastic that shrinks to about 60 percent of its original size when it is baked in the oven or heated with a heat embossing tool. It is available in clear, semiopaque white, white, ivory, brown and black and can be decorated with colored pencils, chalks, markers, crayons and inks, although decorating is usually done before heating. Heated shrink plastic also holds stamped impressions, as you will see in this chapter.

When working with polymer clay and shrink plastic, always follow the manufacturer's guidelines for baking and safety. It is important to work in a well-ventilated area, as the fumes can be irritating. If you happen to burn your clay or plastic, take it outside to cool, then throw it away. It is imperative to dedicate a small toaster oven to polymer clay, and never mix tools used for polymer clay with tools used for food preparation.

RIVER ROCKS

The river rocks in this project are actually scraps of clay left over from other projects. After shaping them, I covered them with a veneer of nice black clay, then coated them with liquid polymer clay. After you bake the rocks, coat them with another layer of liquid polymer clay or heat them with a heat embossing tool for extra shine. The results are equally pleasing. The white acrylic paint is striking against the smooth, black rocks, and the rubber stamped images lend just enough of a tribal feel to make them look like they might have been painted by people from an ancient culture.

MATERIALS

Decorative rubber stamps (JUDIKINS)

1 block of black polymer clay and scrap clay from other projects

Liquid polymer clay

Cardstock

16- and 18-gauge silver wire

White acrylic paint

Foam brush

Tissue blade

Wire cutters

Ruler

Round-nose pliers

Pin vise and ⅛" (3mm) drill bit

Heat embossing tool

Pasta machine

Cookie sheet

➤ Condition one block of black clay by kneading it with your hands until it is soft and workable. Run the clay through the pasta machine on the thickest setting, then fold the sheet in half and run it through several more times, always inserting the fold into the machine first to prevent air bubbles.

▼ Divide a piece of scrap clay into four or five pieces, depending on the desired length for your bracelet, and shape them into rocks. Use a tissue blade to cut the conditioned sheet of clay from step 1 into four or five sheets large enough to cover your scrap clay rocks. Cover the rocks, trim off the excess and smooth out any cracks and bubbles with your fingers.

HELPFUL HINT

Scrap clay probably has to be run through the machine only a few times if you have used it recently. If the clay is brand new, however, I usually run it through about twenty times.

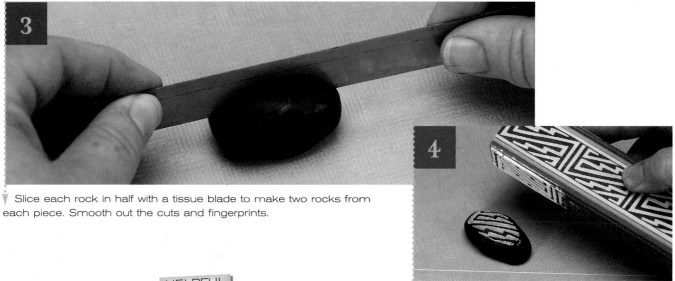

Slice each rock in half with a tissue blade to make two rocks from each piece. Smooth out the cuts and fingerprints.

HELPFUL HINT

To make liquid polyclay extremely shiny, blast it with the heat embossing tool for about five minutes after it has been baked and cooled. Be sure to keep the tool moving evenly over the clay to achieve an even gloss.

Tap white acrylic paint onto a decorative stamp with a foam brush. Stamp onto the clay rocks and allow the paint to dry. Then, apply a coat of liquid polymer clay with your finger.

Using a pin vise with a small drill bit, drill two parallel holes all the way through each rock.

Place a piece of cardstock on a cookie sheet, then arrange the rocks on the cardstock, about 1" (2.5cm) apart. Bake according to manufacturer's instructions. I baked these rocks, which are ½" (1.3cm) thick, at 275°F (135°C) for thirty minutes, allowed them to cool, and then baked them again for another thirty minutes.

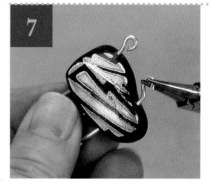

Cut sixteen to twenty pieces of 18-gauge wire measuring the width of your largest river rock plus ½" (1.3cm). Insert the wires through the holes and use round-nose pliers to make loops on the ends. Do not close the loops all the way, as you will use them to link the clay rocks together.

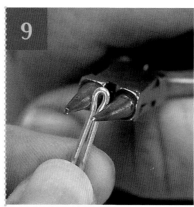

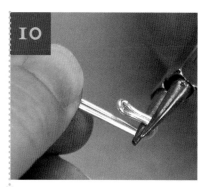

Attach the rocks together with the loops, closing them with your pliers as you go.

To make a hook clasp, cut a 3½" (8.9cm) piece of 18-gauge wire. Grasp the middle of the wire with round-nose pliers and bend down both ends to make a hairpin shape. Use the pliers to pinch the wire on each side of the bend, as shown.

Make a tiny half-loop on the very end of the hairpin, then grasp the wire about ⅜" (1cm) from the half-loop and bend it in the opposite direction.

Pull the legs of the hook apart and use round-nose pliers to make loops face inward, as shown. Fasten the loops to the last rock, then close all the loops.

To make a connector for the hook clasp, cut a 2" (5.1cm) piece of 16-gauge wire. Coil the ends into 1¼" (3.2cm) spirals pointing inward, as shown, and fasten the spirals to the loops on the other end of the bracelet. Close the loops and fasten the bracelet with the hook.

PEYOTE POLY CLAY

Not only does this project use polymer clay and delicate gold leafing, but it also incorporates an easy beading technique called the peyote stitch. This popular, single-needle technique is easier than it looks, so don't let it throw you if you have never done bead stitching before. With a few beads, a needle and thread, you can make an ordinary trinket into an extraordinary treasure brooch. There is very little that is as beautiful and captivating as the swirls of iridescent color and multiple patinas from glass beads. You'll want to make several of these gems for gifts as well as for yourself.

MATERIALS

Decorative
rubber stamps
(RUBBER MOON)

⅛ block each of
black, turquoise,
translucent, pearl,
silver and purple
polymer clay

Liquid polymer clay

Cardstock

Faux suede

Felt

Seed beads

Pinback

Fishing wire (FIRELINE)

Gold leafing

Paintbrush

Acrylic roller

Scissors

Tissue blade

Size 13 beading
needle

Pasta machine

320- and 400-grit
wet/dry sandpaper

Fabri-Tac

Gem-Tac

Cookie sheet

Water in small bowl

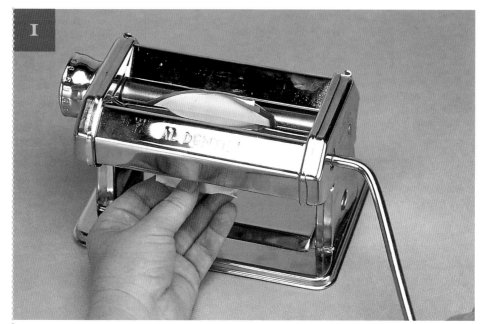

Condition the black, turquoise, translucent, pearl, silver and purple clays. Run each sheet through the thickest setting on the pasta machine and layer the sheets on top of each other in the order listed above. Flatten the stack with an acrylic roller, then roll it through the pasta machine on the thickest setting.

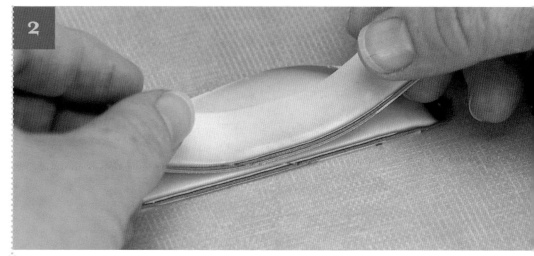

Slice a ½" (1.3cm) wide strip off the stacked sheet with a tissue blade and stack it on top of the remaining sheet. Continue slicing strips and stacking until you have a striped bar of clay.

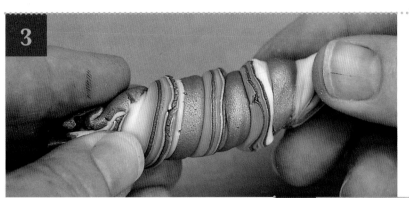

▶ Twist the bar to marble the colors, as shown.

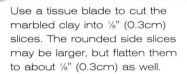

Use a tissue blade to cut the marbled clay into ⅛" (0.3cm) slices. The rounded side slices may be larger, but flatten them to about ⅛" (0.3cm) as well.

▼ Place the slices side by side and blend the seams with your fingers to make one sheet. Run the sheet through the pasta machine on the thickest setting.

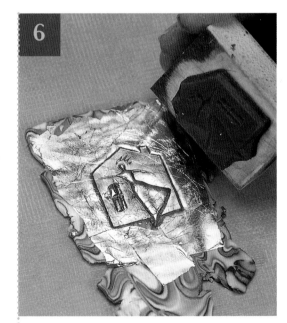

▼ Apply gold leafing over the clay sheet and press with your finger to adhere. Firmly press the stamp into the clay over the gold leafing, then lift to reveal the image.

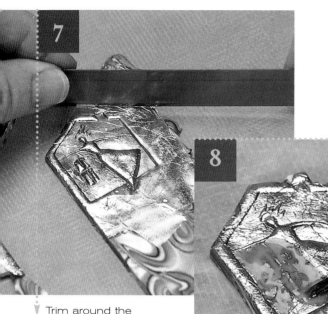

▼ Trim around the stamped image with a tissue blade, saving scrap pieces for other jewelry.

Use a paintbrush to coat the stamped clay with liquid polymer clay, making sure the medium gets inside the stamped impression. Place the stamped clay on a piece of cardstock and bake according to the manufacturer's instructions. Allow it to cool.

▼ Soak 320-grit wet/dry sandpaper in a bowl of water. Use the 320-grit sandpaper to sand off the top layer of liquid polymer clay and gold leafing. Continue dipping the clay and sandpaper in water as you go. Then, use 400-grit sandpaper to smooth any lines made by the first round of sanding. Apply a thin coat of liquid polymer clay and rebake the piece for about fifteen minutes at 275°F (135°C).

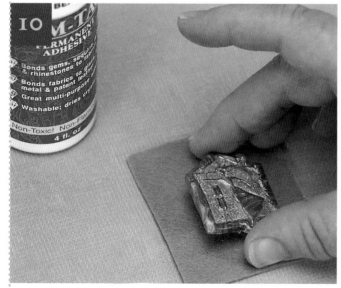

▼ Cut a piece of felt to at least ½" (1.3cm) larger than the stamped clay piece on all sides. Adhere the back of the clay piece to the felt with Gem-Tac. Allow to dry.

▼ Cut about 3 yards (2.75m) of fishing wire. Knot one end of the wire and thread the other end with a beading needle. Sew up through the back of the felt at the bottom right corner of the clay piece.

▶ String three seed beads onto the wire, then sew back down through the felt. Sew back up at the original starting place and thread the needle through the three seed beads.

▶ String three more seed beads onto the wire, then sew back down through the felt and back up at the starting point of the second series of seed beads. Thread the needle through the second series of seed beads, then add three more. Continue this process all the way around the clay piece to complete the first row.

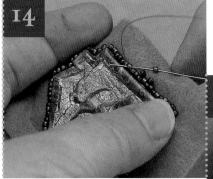

▼ Thread one bead onto the needle, stack it over the first bead in the first row, and pass the needle through the second bead in the first row. Add another seed bead to the needle, stack it over the third bead in the first row, and pass the needle through the fourth bead in the first row. Continue in this manner all the way around the piece.

▼ To complete the third row, fill in the spaces left in the previous row with more beads using the same method.

▼ Once you have made it back to the original starting point for the third time, sew down through the felt and tie a knot in the wire. Trim off the excess wire. Trim all the excess felt away, being careful not to clip any of your stitches. Attach a faux suede pinback as described on page 29.

Thread your needle with 36" (91 cm) of wire. To hide the tail of the wire, slide the needle between the felt and faux suede layers.

To make a border around the back of the pin, string a bead onto the wire, sew down into the two layers of felt, and then sew back up through the bead.

Thread another bead onto the needle, sew down through the felt, then back up through the same bead. Continue in this manner until you are all the way around the back of the clay piece.

When you finish the beaded edging, run the wire ends through the felt layers, knot and trim off. This is how the back of the finished pin will look.

SHRINK BLINKS

The word "blinks" is short for black links. Cute, huh? Anyway, wires embedded between layers of shrink plastic make interesting connectors. My shrink plastic shapes are freeform in these projects, but I often trace and cut out really cool shapes from "shapelets," which are templates designed for use with polymer clay. You can shape your wire connector ends to just about any size or shape you like, but keep the drape of the bracelet in mind. I test each link as I make it to be sure that it has a nice swing and will not get caught up or kink when I wear it.

MATERIALS

Decorative
rubber stamps
(JUDIKINS, HERO ARTS)

Black shrink plastic

Tiny gold beads

Bead tray

18- and 20-
gauge wire

Oval jump rings
(see page 19)

Acrylic paints in
metallic colors

Paintbrushes

Acrylic block or
heavy flat object

Pinking shears

Wire cutters

Round-nose pliers

Chasing hammer
and block

Diamond Glaze

Heat embossing tool

Cut twelve pieces of shrink plastic to approximately 1½" x 2" (3.8cm x 5.1cm) with pinking shears. Heat each piece with a heat embossing tool for about fifteen seconds or until it has stopped shrinking and lays flat.

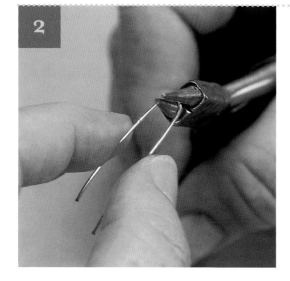

Cut six 3" (7.6cm) pieces of 20-gauge wire. Grasp the middle of one wire with your round-nose pliers and bend down both ends of the wire to make a hairpin shape. Repeat with the remaining wires.

HELPFUL HINT

You can control the flattening shape by pulling the gun away if the plastic heats too fast and curls like it will stick together. Let the plastic cool, flip it over and continue heating.

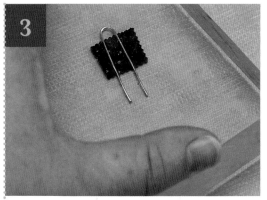

Place one wire across a piece of shrink plastic as shown and heat the piece for about five seconds. Place a heavy object such as an acrylic block on top of it to embed the wire. Allow the plastic to cool while repeating this step with five more pieces of wire and plastic.

Place another piece of shrink plastic over the first piece to sandwich the wire, then reheat for about ten seconds. Impress a decorative stamp into the plastic while it is hot. If you don't get a good stamped impression, reheat the plastic and try it again. Repeat with the remaining five pieces of shrink plastic.

Randomly apply metallic acrylic paints to the raised portions of the stamped plastic pieces and allow them to dry. Do not heat the paint with the heat embossing tool to dry it, as this will remelt the plastic. Apply small amounts of Diamond Glaze with a paintbrush where you want to glue the gold beads.

Pour tiny gold beads onto the plastic pieces and tap off the excess. Let dry. Brush away any excess beads with a dry paintbrush.

Use round-nose pliers to pinch the wire legs sticking out of the shrink plastic pieces in toward the center, then roll both legs forward into a loop, as shown.

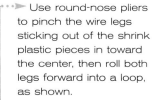

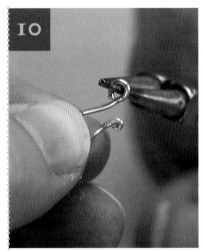

Hook the pieces together as shown, then close the loops with round-nose pliers.

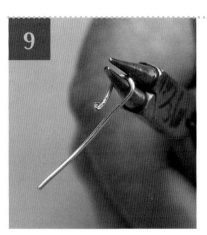

▶ To make a clasp, cut a 1¾" (4.5cm) piece of 18-gauge wire and make a tiny half-loop at one end with round-nose pliers. Grasp the wire about ⅜" (1cm) from the half-loop and bend it around the pliers in the opposite direction. Clip off the wire about ⅜" (1cm) from the end.

▶ Fasten an oval jump ring to the end of the last shrink plastic loop.

Loop the straight end of the wire with the pliers in the opposite direction, as shown. This is essentially an S-clasp, but only one loop is open instead of both. Place the clasp on the chasing block and flatten it with a chasing hammer.

▶ Attach the clasp to the oval jump ring and to the other end of the bracelet.

CHARMING ADORNMENTS

Chock full of dangles or as simple as can be—either way, one-of-a-kind trinkets make this a fascinating art piece. You will probably need to set aside the good part of a day to complete this bracelet. With a handmade, linked chain and many colorful, wire-wrapped charms, this project is a little labor-intense. Add colorful glass beads and you will see that it is well worth your effort with all the "oohs" and "aahs" you'll get. Make tiny charms with smaller beads and attach findings for a sizzling set of earrings. Or, how about making a series of looped charms to dangle off the end of a long chain for a unique pendant? The list of projects that you can make with these charms goes on and on.

MATERIALS

Decorative
rubber stamps
(JUDIKINS, HERO ARTS,
STAMPOTIQUE)

White shrink plastic

Assorted decorative
beads

Seed beads

Bead tray

18-, 20- and 22-
gauge wire

Dye re-inkers

Paintbrush

Small paint palette

¼" (0.6cm) dowel

Pinking shears

Wire cutters

Round-nose pliers

Chasing block
and hammer

Diamond Glaze

Heat embossing tool

Use pinking shears to cut fifty to sixty pieces of white shrink plastic into random shapes about 1½" x 2¼" (3.8cm x 5.7cm). Heat in the oven at 250°F (121°C) for about one minute, or until the pieces have shrunk and flattened back out. Arrange the pieces into pairs of similar size and shape. Heat one piece for about ten seconds with a heat embossing tool, then impress with a decorative stamp. Hold the stamp down with firm pressure for a few seconds while it cools, then lift the stamp to see the impressed image.

HELPFUL HINT

When making a
large number
of shrink plastic
pieces, it is quicker
to shrink them all
at once by baking
them in the oven
on a cookie sheet.
Use a heat gun
to remelt each
piece, then impress
with a stamp.

Cut twenty-five 4" (10.2cm) pieces of 22-gauge wire. Flip the stamped plastic piece and heat for just a few seconds, then place a piece of wire on the plastic. Place the matching plastic piece over the wire, heat and stamp to impress the image and melt the pieces together. Repeat with the remaining shrink plastic and wires. You'll need a minimum of two pieces of shrink plastic and one wire for each charm.

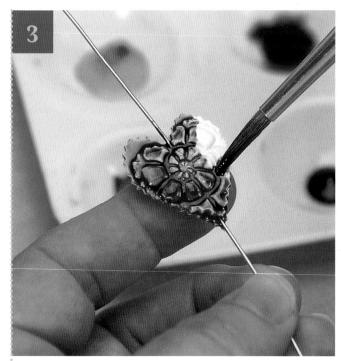

To make figure-eight bracelet links, cut a 15" to 20" (3.8cm x 5.1cm) length of 20-gauge wire and wrap it around a ¼" (0.6cm) dowel. Pull the coil off the dowel. Count two loops, then clip with wire cutters, count two more, then cut again. Repeat to make about seven two-loop sections. You may need more or less, depending on the desired length of your bracelet.

Mix about ⅛ tablespoon of Diamond Glaze with a drop of dye re-inker on the paint palette. Repeat for the desired number of colors. Paint the Diamond Glaze mixture onto the stamped plastic pieces and blend with a paintbrush. Set aside to dry.

Open each two-loop section with your fingers, as shown.

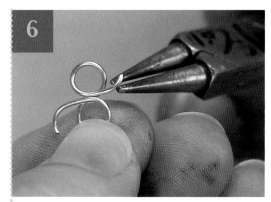

Flatten each two-loop section into a figure-eight with your fingers. Holding the bottom of the figure-eight, use round-nose pliers to pull the legs out and curl them into tiny loops, as shown. Repeat with the remaining two-loop sections. Flatten the pieces on the chasing block with the hammer.

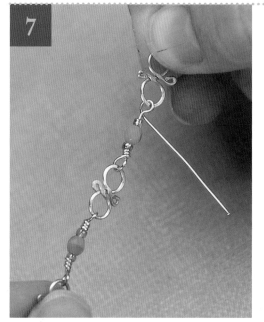

Cut five to eight 3" (7.6cm) pieces of 22-gauge wire and use round-nose pliers to loop one end of each wire to form eyepins. (For instructions, see page 17.) Attach one of the eyepins to a figure-eight link from step 6. String the eyepin with one seed bead, one decorative bead and one seed bead. Make a loop at the end of the eyepin and attach it to another figure-eight link. Wrap the remaining wire from the eyepin around the pin, just above the seed bead. Repeat until the desired bracelet length is achieved.

To make a figure-eight closure with 18-gauge wire, keep the wire on the spool (to reduce waste) and make a tiny loop at the end of the wire with round-nose pliers. Then, make a larger loop, wrapping in the opposite direction, as shown. Cut the wire at the end of second loop. Flatten it on a chasing block with a chasing hammer and attach the small loop to one end of the chain.

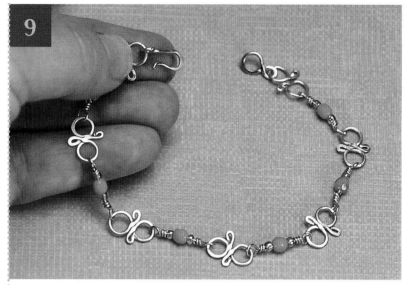

Make a hook clasp as described on page 75, steps 9–11 and attach it to the other end of the chain. Curl the legs into tiny loops as you did in step 6. This makes a cute bracelet, even without the charms!

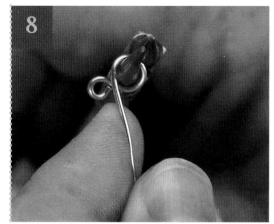

Retrieve the dry shrink plastic pieces from step 3 and string decorative beads onto the bottom wires. Bend the wires into decorative shapes such as triangles and spirals.

Thread a couple of beads onto the top wires, then attach them to the links in the chain with round-nose pliers, spacing them evenly. You can trim the excess wires flush to the wrap or loop and bend them decoratively.

Cut several more pieces of 22-gauge wire, crimp one end of each wire and string with decorative beads to make bead dangles. Attach the bead dangles to the links of the bracelet with round-nose pliers and bend or trim the excess wires as desired.

REVERSIBLE SHRINKY LINKS

When you punch shapes from shrink plastic, you are left with the "positive" punched out shape and the "negative" left-over plastic. Never one to waste art supplies, I discovered that if I cut around the negatives with pinking shears, I would end up with very usable links. For this project, I decorated both sides of each plastic piece to coordinate with each other, but you could also make two completely different sides for a reversible bracelet. The macramé in this project consists of simply passing left and right cords, called working cords, through and around a center cord, called the post. Macramé is much easier when you pin your cords to a working board. I use foam core board.

MATERIALS

Decorative
rubber stamps
(JudiKins)

White shrink plastic

Foam core board

Oval beads

Thin gold cord

Chalk inks in
various colors

Black permanent
marker

Pinking shears

Large decorative
hole punch

Corsage pin

Tiny crochet hook

Diamond glaze

Heat embossing tool

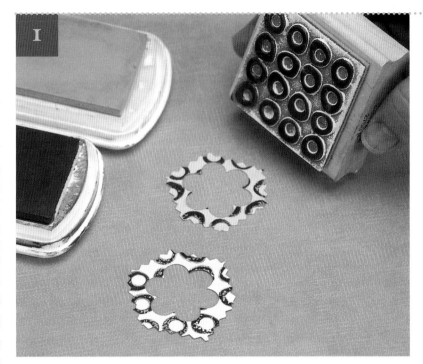

Use a large decorative hole punch to punch out shapes from a piece of white shrink plastic. Set the positive pieces aside for use in another project. Cut around the holes in the negative pieces with pinking shears. Apply chalk ink by wiping the inkpad onto the plastic. Color around the edges with black permanent marker if desired. Apply chalk ink to decorative stamps and stamp onto both sides of the plastic. Heat each piece with a heat embossing tool for about fifteen seconds to shrink it.

Apply a thin coat of Diamond Glaze to one side of each piece and allow it to dry, then flip it over and coat the other side. Set the pieces aside to dry.

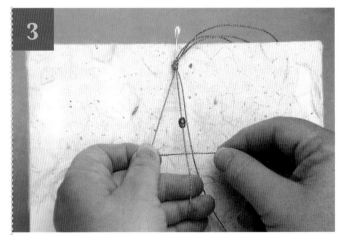

Cut three pieces of gold cord to four or five times the size of your wrist and bundle them together. Tie a knot in the cords, about 6" (15.2cm) from one end. Pin the knot to the top of your foam core board with a corsage pin. String an oval bead onto the center post, then curve the left working cord over the post to form the number 4.

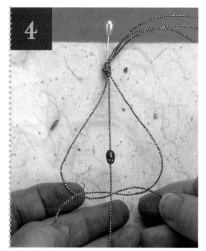

▼ Position the right cord over the tail of the left cord, then bring it behind the post and through the loop. Pull taut. You have essentially tied an overhand knot around the post string.

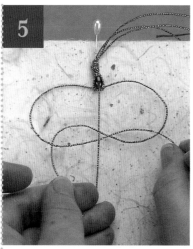

▼ Follow step 4 in reverse, making a backwards number 4 with the right cord, positioning the left cord over the tail of the right cord, bringing it behind the post and through the loop. Pull taut to complete a square knot under the bead.

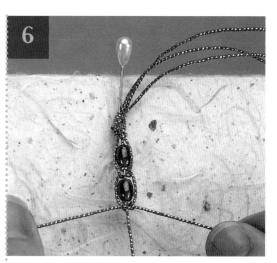

▼ String another oval bead onto the post and repeat steps 3–5.

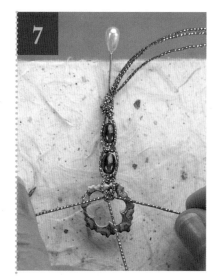

▼ String one of the shrink charms from step 2 onto the post through the punched out hole and repeat steps 3–5, securing the link with a square knot.

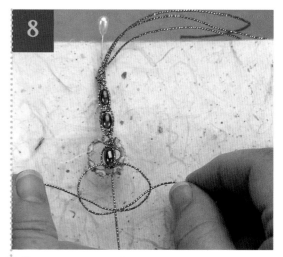

▼ String another oval bead onto the post and repeat steps 3 and 4. Thread the post back through the hole in the shrink charm, leaving your left and right cords at the front of the charm, then repeat step 5.

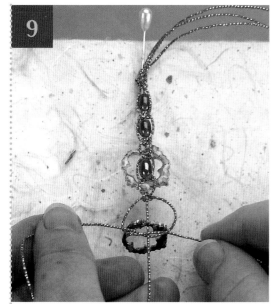

▽ Repeat steps 3 and 4, then lay a shrink charm down on all three cords. Pull the post through the hole in the charm, then repeat step 5. Continue the oval bead, knot, shrink charm, knot sequence until you have reached your desired length. End with two oval beads as you began.

▽ To make an adjustable closure, first separate the post on each end of the bracelet and overlap them as shown.

▽ Trim the ends of the working cords to about ½" (1.3cm) and use a fine crochet hook to weave the remaining ½" (1.3cm) in and out of the square knots.

▽ Tie four square knots with the working cords on one end of the bracelet, enclosing the overlapping posts. Repeat with the working cords on the other end of the bracelet, also enclosing the overlapping posts. Be sure to keep the post ends extended beyond the square knot. They will be your pull-ties.

Tie oval beads to the end of each post. Pull the bracelet to make it larger, or pull the beaded posts to tighten it.

Metalworks

Metal working can seem intimidating at times. I know it was tough for me. I would read a book and just be inundated with way too much information for my brain to digest. I would give up and only dream of the day that I would have time to learn it all. Well, guess what? It turns out that much of it is easy after all! There was just too much jargon blinding my way to creativity. This chapter will give you a stripped down and fun version of metal working.

Most of the projects in this chapter require soldering. This may sound intimidating, but it is really simple and quite fun. Make a quick trip to your local hardware, hobby or jewelry supply store to load up on the necessary supplies (see page 14 for details), and you'll be ready to go.

One project also requires the use of a torch. Before you cower in fear like I did, let me reassure you that it is also extremely easy. The premise of soldering is that both pieces of metal must get hot enough for the solder to flow between them. If the metal does not get hot enough with a soldering iron, a torch will heat the metal to the desired temperature.

Remember to always use flux and solder in a well-ventilated area. If you plan on burning enamel off metal with a torch, wear a mask to avoid inhaling airborne particles and burn in a well-ventilated area—or outside if at all possible. Also, remember that soldered metal and soldering tools get hot! Don't touch them with your bare hands until they have had time to cool down. Finally, always wear leather gloves when you cut sheet metal. I recommend getting a pair of scissors that are used strictly for cutting metal so you won't ruin your good scissors.

COLLAGED PIN

I think you'll agree that this design is fun, easy and beautiful. The base of the pin is a piece of tumbled stained glass called ClinkIts! You can get these glass pieces from Alicia G. Creative (see the Resources section on pages 124–125). Each piece of glass is hand cut, tumbled and sanded to remove the rough edges, so no two pieces are identical in size or shape. I often apply copper tape to the edges of glass pieces to add a decorative quality. The flattened metal ring also adds an element of interest to this pin. I am always finding metal rings like the one in this project at thrift stores and garage sales. They are perfect for smashing flat and using as unique embellishments.

MATERIALS

Decorative
rubber stamp
(STAMP OASIS)

Face rubber stamp
(STAMPINGTON & CO.)

Glass piece (ClinkIts!
by Alicia G. Creative)

Clear flat-backed
marble

White cardstock

Feather

Assorted decorative
beads

Metal ring

Metal star

Pinback

20-gauge wire

Copper tape

Black solvent ink

Scissors

Wire cutters

Crimping and
round-nose pliers

Chasing block
and hammer

Gem-Tac

Permanent adhesive
for glass and metal

Ink a decorative stamp with black solvent ink and impress it onto a piece of glass.

Apply copper tape to the bottom edge of the glass and pinch on both sides to secure.

Wrap the copper tape all the way around the glass, overlapping the seam at the bottom by about ⅛" (0.3cm) and trim off the excess. Pinch the tape in the center, then all the way around the edges. Burnish the tape with the side of a marker.

Ink the face stamp with black solvent ink and stamp it onto white cardstock.

Trim the stamped face to slightly smaller than the back of a clear, flat-backed marble. Adhere the face to the flat back with Gem-Tac.

Open the metal ring, place it on the chasing block and flatten it with the chasing hammer.

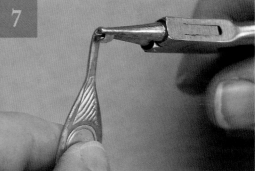

Curl one end of the flattened ring with round-nose pliers, as shown.

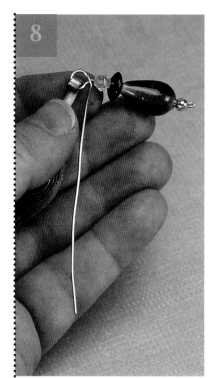

▶ Apply permanent adhesive for glass and metal to the back of the metal ring and adhere it to the glass piece, as shown.

▼ Cut a 6" (15cm) piece of 20-gauge wire and flatten one end with crimping pliers to make it into a headpin. String decorative beads onto the wire, then loop the wire through the curl in the flattened metal ring. Wrap the excess wire around the neck of the bead dangle and trim off any excess. Tuck the end of the wire flat against the neck of the dangle.

▶ Adhere the feather, star and the marble over the ring with Gem-Tac. Do not use the glass and metal adhesive for this step, as it may dissolve the stamped image.

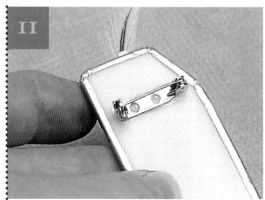

▼ To finish, flip the piece over and adhere a pinback with glass and metal adhesive.

METAL PETALS

I found this wire mesh at an electronics surplus store. I held onto it for a couple of years, thinking that it would make some sort of fabulous bracelet, but I never did anything with it until I learned to solder. Then, Metal Petals just kind of fell into place. This mesh is usually used to bundle several electronic wires together. For this project, I've used copper, brass and silver craft wire to match the petals to the silver mesh. Another more colorful option would be to use colored craft wire to make the petals. Then you could lay out your design, put a spot of masking tape over the places where you want to solder and spray-paint the mesh. I can picture all sorts of exciting things happening here!

MATERIALS

Decorative
rubber stamps
(JudiKins, Stamp Oasis)

Silver wire mesh

Faux suede scraps

Seed beads

Wooden buttons and
metal washers

Flat necklace clasp

Jump rings

Lobster claw clasp

18- and 20-gauge
gold, silver and
copper wires

Fishing wire

Black solvent ink

Black permanent
marker

White marker

Scissors

Wire cutters

Chain-nose pliers

Chasing block and
hammer

Size 13 beading
needle

Dowels, markers and
knitting needles in
various diameters

Flux

Soldering iron and
solder

Heat sink

Damp sponge

Fabri-Tac

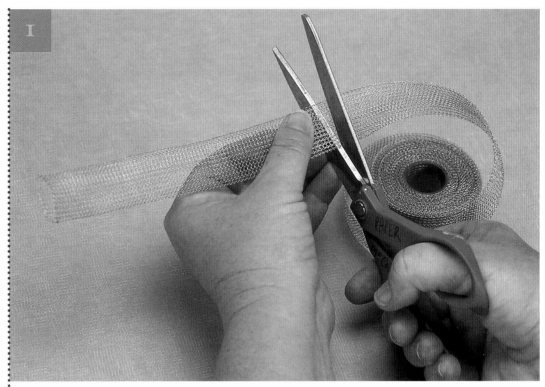

▼ Cut a piece of wire mesh to about the size of your wrist minus ½" (1.3cm).

▶ Fold both ends in
about ⅛" (0.3cm).

HELPFUL
HINT

Do you see me
cutting wire with
paper scissors?
Sometimes you
just forget. I use
a Fiskars scissor
sharpener to
get my scissors
back in shape.
It'll even get your
fabric scissors in
working order
after you've used
them to cut paper.

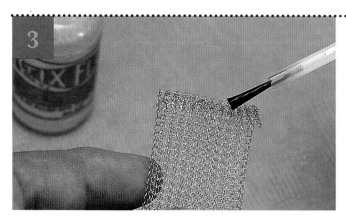

► Brush a generous amount of flux onto the folded areas of the mesh, where you will be soldering. Apply flux to the jewelry findings at the points where they will be attached to the mesh, as well. The flux will clean the pieces and give them a little bit of "tooth," allowing the solder to stick to the fluxed areas. Place one of the jewelry findings on the heat sink and position the folded area of the wire mesh over it.

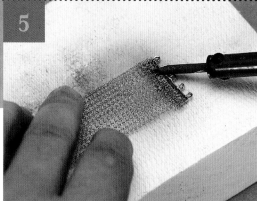

► Touch the tip of the hot soldering iron to the end of the solder until a little ball of solder forms on the hot iron. The solder will melt and stick to the tip of the iron.

► Touch the tip of the soldering iron to the finding and mesh to solder them together. Repeat with the other end of the mesh and the other finding. Do not move for about two seconds so that the solder can cool and your joint is made.

HELPFUL HINT

For easy tinning, many soldering irons come with sponges built into the holder.

▼ Clean your soldering iron by running it across a damp sponge after each solder. This process, called tinning, will remove any excess flux and ash from the iron.

Cut several 8" (20.3cm) pieces of 18- and 20-gauge wire in gold, silver and copper.

Wrap the wires around various objects such as dowels, markers and knitting needles to get coils of different diameters and colors.

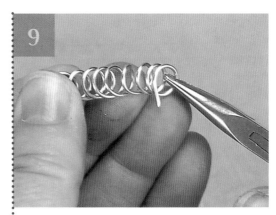

Remove the wires and compress the coils down and to the side. Holding one side of one of the coils with your fingers and the other with chain-nose pliers, pull out the coils, as shown. Cut the coil into five-loop pieces.

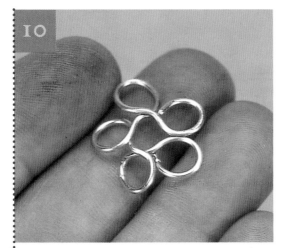

Bend and twist each loop about 45° to make petals. Continue bending and twisting until you have the desired flower shape. Cut off any excess coil.

Place the flowers on the chasing block and flatten them with the chasing hammer.

12

Use a black permanent marker to mark the desired placement of the flowers on the mesh. (This is so you won't lose your spot when you are soldering from the back side.)

HELPFUL HINT

If you accidentally solder something to the wrong spot, touch the hot iron to the spot and it will melt the solder. Just be sure to reflux before you resolder.

13

Apply flux to the front and back of the mesh on the marks. Apply more flux to the back of the flower.

14

Place a flower on the heat sink, then place the mesh bracelet over it. Solder the pieces together through the mesh as described in steps 4 and 5, pressing down on the flower with chain-nose pliers to keep it from moving.

15

Ink a decorative stamp with black solvent ink and stamp it onto the wooden buttons and metal washers.

16

Color in the highlights with a white marker.

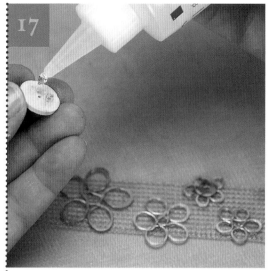

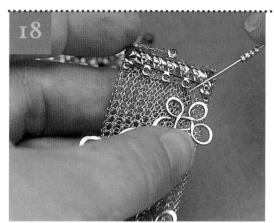

Thread a needle with fishing wire and tie a knot at the end. Sew through the back side of the mesh near one of the flowers. String a few seed beads onto the thread, then sew back down through the mesh. Continue in this manner to sew seed beads around the flowers as desired. Put a dab of superglue over the string knots.

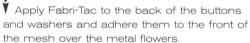 Apply Fabri-Tac to the back of the buttons and washers and adhere them to the front of the mesh over the metal flowers.

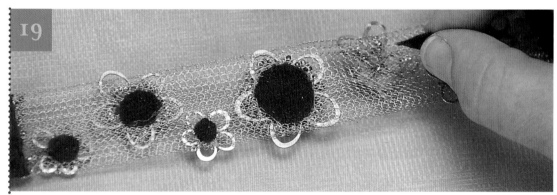

Cut out little pieces from scraps of faux suede and glue them to the back of the mesh to cover the soldered joints.

Use chain-nose pliers to attach jump rings to both ends of the bracelet on the jewelry findings. Attach the lobster claw clasp or the clasp of your choice to the jump rings.

BEAUTIFUL BEZEL

The bezels in this project are made of base metal, but you can get them through just about any jewelry supply catalog in any type of metal. I bought a ton of these at a garage sale because I thought they would surely be useful for something. Since then, I have been having fun filling them with everything from fabric to foam core to concrete! In this project, you'll see that I use Helping Hands. This is an inexpensive tool that holds small parts in place while you solder, glue or even paint them. You'll find it in hobby stores, craft stores, jewelry-making supply catalogs and in some hardware stores.

MATERIALS

Decorative
rubber stamps
(HERO ARTS, JUDIKINS)

Plain white paper

Mat board

Assorted decorative
beads

Metal bezel

Clamshells

Jump rings
(see page 18)

Spring-loaded
necklace clasp

Nylon beading cord

16-, 20- and 22-
gauge wire

Orange and red dye
inks

Gold pigment ink

Black solvent ink

Pen

Craft knife

Scissors

Wire cutters

Chain-nose,
crimping and
round-nose pliers

Helping Hands

Chasing block and
hammer

Flux

Soldering iron
and solder

Diamond Glaze

Fabri-Tac

Superglue

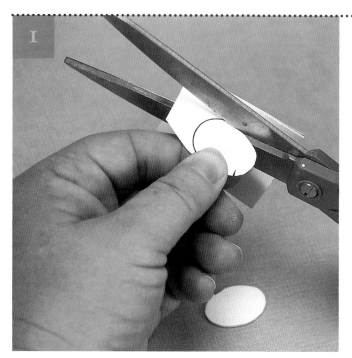

▶ Trace the metal bezel two times onto a piece of mat board. Cut one piece of board just a hair inside the traced line so that it will fit inside the metal bezel. Cut the other piece approximately ⅛" (0.3cm) inside the traced line.

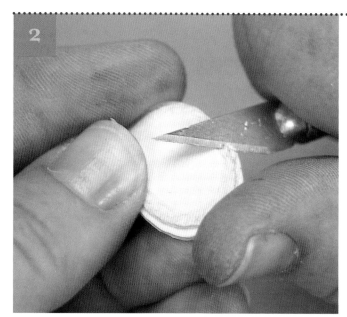

▶ Glue the pieces of mat board together with Fabri-Tac and round the edges of the smaller piece of mat board with a craft knife.

▼ Decorate a piece of plain white paper with red and orange dye inks. Ink a decorative stamp with black ink and stamp randomly onto the paper.

▼ Ink another decorative stamp with gold pigment ink and stamp over the other images. Use a heat gun to dry all the inks.

▼ Place the metal bezel on the stamped paper, trace the outline and cut it out, this time cutting just outside the traced line. Set these pieces aside while you prepare the bezel.

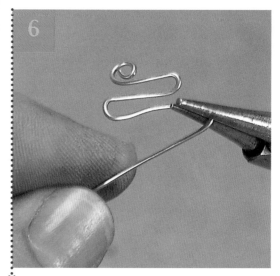

▼ Keeping it on the spool, bend a piece of 20-gauge wire into a squiggle shape with round-nose pliers. When you have the desired shape, cut it off the spool and coil the ends. Lay the wire on the chasing block and flatten it with the chasing hammer. This will be your dangle holder.

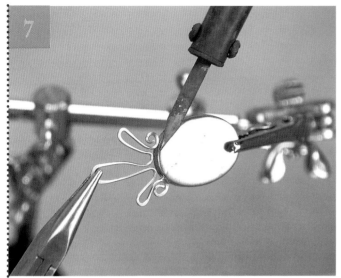

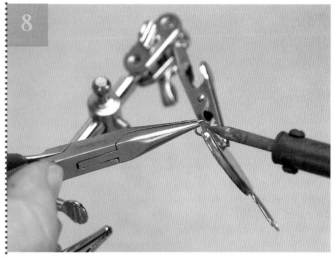

▼ Apply flux to the bottom of the metal bezel and to the points on the wire where you want them to join. Place the bezel in the helping hands and hold the wire in your nondominant hand with chain-nose pliers. Hold the soldering iron in your dominant hand and touch the tip of the iron to the solder until a little ball of solder forms on the hot iron. Touch the iron onto the wire where it meets the bezel and watch the solder flow. Hold the wire to the bezel for about two seconds so that the solder can cool.

▼ Flux and solder a jump ring to the top of the bezel, with the seam of the jump ring against the bezel. Make sure to flux the inside of the jump ring as well as the outside. Touch the solder-laden iron to the inside of the jump ring where it meets the bezel and hold it there until the iron heats both pieces and the solder flows to make a good connection.

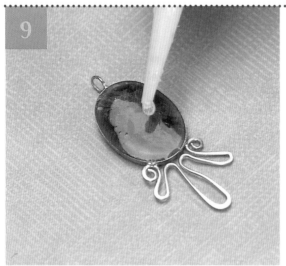

▶ Use Fabri-Tac to glue the cut-out decorative paper from step 5 over the mat board bezel from step 2 and place it in the palm of your hand. Press it down with a pen to shape it into a dome. Glue it in place in the metal bezel and apply Diamond Glaze seal and coat the paper. Let dry completely before going on to the next step.

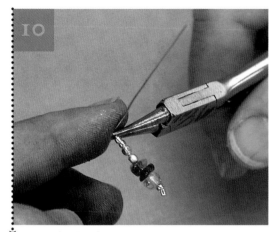

Cut a 3" (7.6cm) piece of 22-gauge wire and crimp the end with crimping pliers to make a headpin. String decorative beads onto the wire to make a dangle, then use round-nose pliers to bond it at a 45° angle.

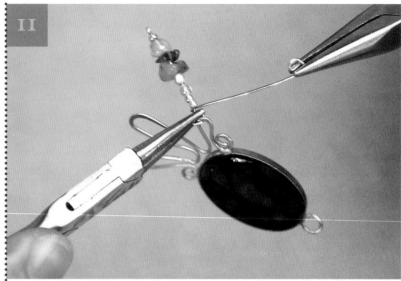

String the dangle onto the wire at the bottom of the metal bezel and wrap the remaining wire around the neck of the dangle two or three times. Trim the excess wire and use crimping pliers to tuck it in close to the neck of the dangle. Repeat to make and attach the desired number of dangles.

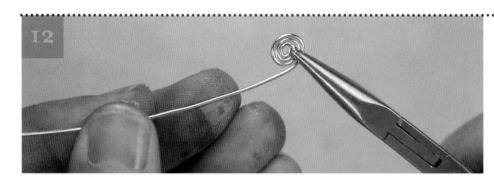

Cut a 10" (25.4cm) piece of 16-gauge wire. Starting on one end, make a spiral about ½" (1.3cm) in diameter with chain-nose pliers.

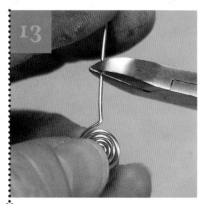

When you have finished the spiral, bend the remaining wire back 90°, as shown. Cut off the end, leaving about ½" (1.3cm) of wire remaining.

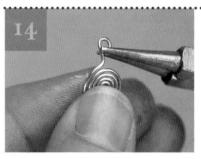

Loop the end of the wire in the opposite direction with round-nose pliers. Use Diamond Glaze to adhere the spiral to the bezel so that the loop sticking up is on top. See step 16 for a close-up view. Let dry.

15

▶ Cut a piece of nylon beading cord to the desired necklace length plus about 4" (10.2cm). Add a clamshell to one end, as described on page 21. Add drops of superglue to the ends of the cord to keep them from fraying, then string beads as desired until you get to the center of the cord.

16

▶ String the bezel onto the cord, running the cord through the jump ring. Continue beading until you reach the end of the cord. Add another clamshell.

HELPFUL HINT

17

▼ String another cord with beads and add clamshells to both ends. Then attach the bead strands to a two-strand clasp like the one shown here.

If the necklace cord is long enough to fit over your head, you don't need to add a clasp.

EMBOSSED BEZEL BRACELET

I love the look of mixed beads and cord together. Just about anything goes as a band for this bracelet. Think chains, cords, leather—the list goes on and on. Even though it looks like a hodgepodge of things that are just thrown together, it isn't. To achieve a pleasing balance, I first laid my beads out on a beading design board. These boards are inexpensive, found at most beading or craft stores and are a boon if you want to save time by seeing the design before you string it. I also love the look that is achieved with embossing ink and powder. It really makes this piece pop.

MATERIALS

Decorative
rubber stamps
(STAMP OASIS)

Mat board

Assorted decorative
beads

Beading design board
(optional)

Metal bezel

Clamshells

Crimp tube with
connector

Jump rings
(see page 18)

Toggle clasp

Leather cord

Nylon beading cord

Black solvent ink

Embossing ink and
embossing powders
in assorted colors

Black permanent
marker

Paintbrush

Craft knife

Scissors

Wire cutters

Chain-nose and
crimping pliers

Helping Hands

Heat embossing tool

Flux

Soldering iron
and solder

Fabri-Tac

Superglue

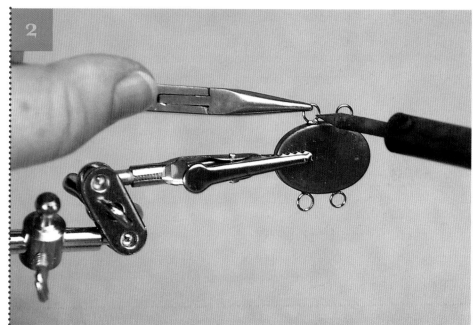

> Follow steps 1 and 2 on page 107 to make a mat board bezel. Use Fabri-Tac to glue it in place on the metal bezel. Use a black permanent marker to mark two evenly spaced dots on each side of the metal bezel. This will mark the placement of your jump rings.

▼ Apply flux to the jump rings at the seams, then apply more flux to the sides of the bezel at the marks. Position the bezel in the helping hands, hold the jump rings with chain-nose pliers in your nondominant hand and the soldering iron in your dominant hand. Solder the pieces together.

► Coat the bezel with embossing ink. Use a paintbrush to get the ink into the cracks if necessary.

▼ Sprinkle embossing powder over the bezel and heat with a heat embossing tool for a few seconds.

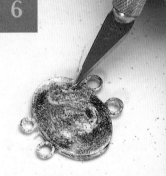

► While the bezel is still hot, apply a few more layers of embossing powder in different colors, heating between each layer.

HELPFUL HINT

If you want a cleaner look to your jewelry, use a baby wipe to clean excess flux from the piece and use tape to protect the jump rings from embossing powder.

▼ Swirl the powder around with a craft knife for a marbled look. Allow it to dry.

7

▶ Ink a decorative stamp with black solvent ink and stamp on top of the bezel over the cooled embossing.

8

▶ Cut a piece of leather cord to about the size of your wrist. Thread the cord through a crimp tube with a connector loop. The connector loop will allow the clasp to be attached to the jump rings on the bezel in the next step.

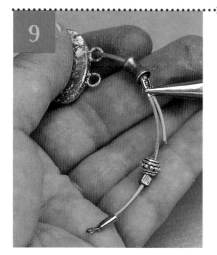

9

▶ String decorative beads onto the leather cord. Thread the cord through a jump ring on the bezel, then back down through the crimp tube. Crimp the tube around the cord with crimping pliers. Cut the cord flush with the crimp tube.

10

▼ Cut a piece of nylon cord to 10" (25cm) and add a clamshell to one end. Thread assorted beads onto the cord until it is the same length as the leather strap that you just made. Add a clamshell to the other end of the cord. Attach to the bezel and then connect both straps to a toggle clasp attached to a soldered jump ring. Repeat steps 8–10 for the other side of the bezel.

PRIMITIVE PIECE

This funky chicken stamp is one of my all-time favorites, but you can also use other stamped art, photographs or pieces of cool vintage postcards. The dog tag in this project is made of a type of metal that does not get hot enough for the solder to flow with just a soldering iron, so I had to use a torch. But don't worry; it's just as easy as using a soldering iron. Another technique demonstrated in this project is setting an eyelet. An eyelet is a metal ring that is inserted into a hole and secured in place with an eyelet setter, which looks like a pen with a rounded tip at one end, and a hammer. A great place to get thin scrap metal is from cookie tins. You can find these in thrift shops, and they are very inexpensive. Sharp craft scissors will cut right through them, but be very careful because the edges will be extremely sharp. I recommend filing them down with a metal file.

MATERIALS

Rubber stamp
(PICTURE SHOW)

Sheet of clear acetate

Scrap of thin metal

White cardstock

Assorted decorative
beads

Metal dog tag with ⅛"
(0.3cm) hole

Large jump ring
(see page 18)

Ball chain

⅛" (0.3cm) eyelet
and eyelet setter

20-gauge wire

Black solvent ink

Watercolor crayons

White gel pen

Black permanent
marker

Paintbrush

Craft scissors

Sharp scissors
dedicated to
cutting metal

Wire cutters

Chain-nose and
round-nose pliers

Miniature clamp or
Helping Hands

Chasing block
and hammer

Awl or nail

Metal file

Flux

Soldering iron
and solder

Torch

400-grit sandpaper

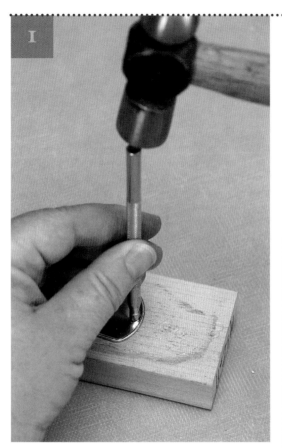

▶ Insert the metal eyelet through the hole in the front of the dog tag. Flip the tag over and position the tip of the eyelet setter into the hole. Pound the end of the setter with the hammer a few times to curl the eyelet down, then remove the setter.

▼ Flip the tag over again and and give the eyelet one more whack with the hammer to secure it.

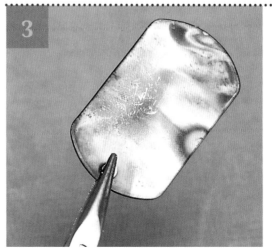

▶ Grasp the dog tag in your chain-nose pliers and hold it over a torch or an open flame for a few seconds to get a burned look.

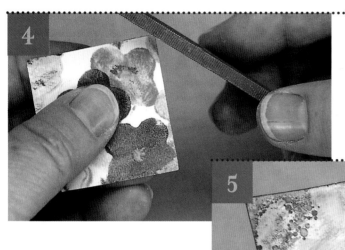

► Use sharp scissors or metal shears to cut a piece of scrap tin, brass or your choice of metal to about 1½" x 1½" (3.8cm x 3.8cm), or large enough so that it extends over the edges of the dog tag. File off the sharp edges with a metal file.

► Grasp the metal scrap with your chain-nose pliers and hold it over a torch or an open flame for a few seconds to burn off the finish. Remember: do not inhale the burning lacquer, and work outside if possible.

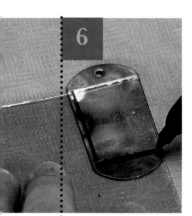

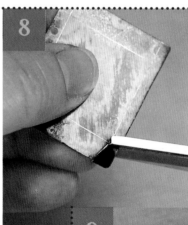

► Cut a little wedge into each corner of the metal with sharp scissors.

▼ Place a piece of thin clear acetate over the dog tag and use a black permanent marker to draw a rectangle about the size of the inside of the dog tag. Cut out the plastic piece with craft scissors.

▼ Place the acetate over the metal scrap and use an awl or nail to scratch the outline of the acetate piece into the metal.

▼ Use chain-nose pliers to fold the metal edges around the acetate to make a frame. Remove the acetate piece.

10 Sand the front of the dog tag and the back of the metal frame with 400-grit sandpaper to remove excess varnish and enamel that may be on the metal. Clean each piece with a solvent-based stamp cleaner. Apply flux to the sanded and cleaned side of each piece.

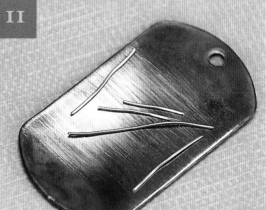

11 Cut several pieces of solder and lay them on the dog tag, as shown.

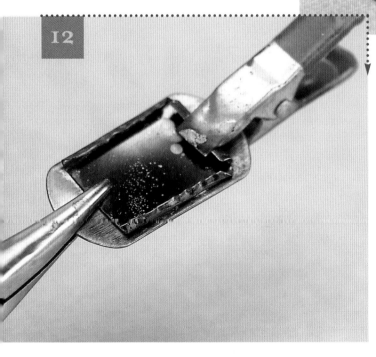

12 Place the back of the metal frame against the front of the dog tag to sandwich the solder pieces. Clamp one end with a miniature clamp or your Helping Hands and hold the other end with your chain-nose pliers. Torch the dog tag from underneath to melt the solder. When the piece flattens out, you'll know that the solder wire has turned to liquid. Take the heat away, but keep the piece clamped until cool.

13 Ink the stamp with black solvent ink and stamp it onto white cardstock.

► Color the image with watercolor crayons and highlight with white gel pen.

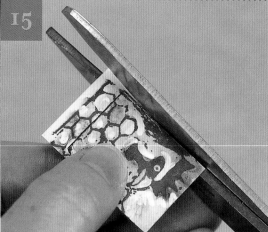

► Cut the stamped image to fit the acetate piece.

▼ Make dimples (tiny indentations) in the dog tag by hammering the tip of an awl or nail into the surface of the tin.

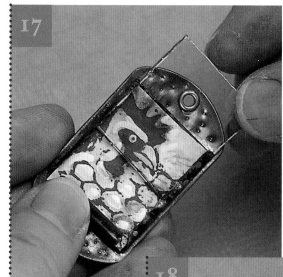

▼ Use chain-nose pliers to open the top side of the frame. Slide the chicken image and plastic into the frame.

▼ Pinch the frame with chain-nose pliers to close it.

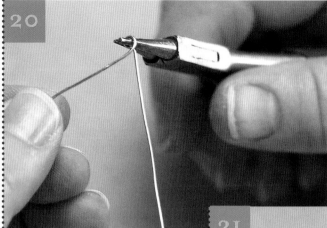

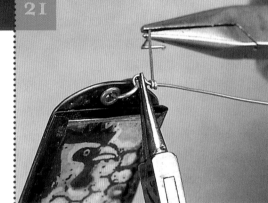

▼ Insert a large jump ring through the eyelet in the dog tag. Apply flux to the jump ring and solder it closed.

▼ Cut a 10" (25.4cm) piece of 20-gauge wire and bend it at a 45° angle about 2" (5.1cm) from the end. Twist the wire around your round-nose pliers to make a loop.

▼ Thread the loop onto the jump ring and wrap the excess short end of the wire around the neck of the wire a couple of times. Trim the wire and tuck in the end.

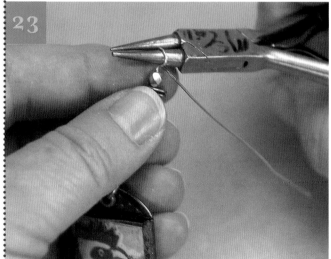

▼ String decorative beads onto the remaining long end of the wire.

▼ To finish the necklace, use round-nose pliers to make a large loop with the excess wire from the dangle. This loop should be large enough to accommodate a ball chain. Wrap the excess wire around the top of the dangle, trim it and tuck in the end. String the dangle onto a ball chain or a chain of your choice.

GALLERY

Need more ideas and inspiration? Take a look at these pieces that are made using the same techniques you learned throughout the book.

Button Blanks Revisited

This simple bracelet is made with only one button blank, glass beads, wire and scrap chain. Note the free-form clasp— any shape you make and like is the perfect shape for a clasp.

Get a Glue: Confessions

Sometimes you'll want part of a stamped image to stand out a little more—especially in a case like this where the text is stamped into hot glue. Just use a permanent fine-tip marker to trace the image for additional impact.

Charming Adornment Pin

The bracelet project on page 86 is the jumping-off point for this pin. Cut several larger pieces of shrink plastic, heat them, and layer them together with wire. Add beads and bend the wire any way you like. Attach a pin-back, and you're good to go!

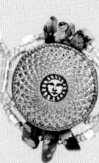

Black Buttoned Bracelet

The beads in any of the projects in this book can be as colorful as you like. As you can see, even plain black and white is very effective.

River Rocks Necklace

The polymer clay rock from the project on page 72 looks right at home in this necklace made of various delicate beads.

Button Blank Bracelet

For this bracelet I used red connector beads between the buttons. Just about any bead works as long as it has holes large enough for the wire to pass through several times.

Bezel Bracelet

Nothing says your beading needs to be symmetrical. Here I varied the beads on each of the four segments of the bracelet band.

Charming Adornment Earrings

Make earrings to match the bracelet on page 86 by using tiny pieces of shrink plastic. You can drill holes in the bottom of the plastic to make chandelier-style earrings.

RESOURCES

Most of the supplies in this book are readily available through art, craft, electronics and jewelry supply stores. If you have difficulty locating any of these materials, refer to this list of manufacturers who will direct you to a supplier in your area.

Alicia G. Creative
2100 Roswell Road
Suite 200C-207
Marietta, GA 30062-0807
www.aliciag.com
· ClinkIts! glass art

American Crafts
476 North 1500 West
Orem, UT 84057
(801) 226-0747
www.americancrafts.com
· Galaxy markers

Artisan's Choice
2066 Wineridge Place
Escondido, CA 92029
(877) 727-8472
www.artisanschoice.com
· Make-your-own stamp kits

Beacon Adhesives Co. Inc.
125 South MacQuesten Parkway
Mount Vernon, KY 10550
(914) 699-3400
www.beacon1.com
· Fabri-Tac, Gem-Tac, Glass,
 Metal and more adhesives

Berkley
1900 18th Street
Spirit Lake, IA 51360
www.berkley-fishing.com
· FireLine fishing wire

Clearsnap, Inc.
P.O. Box 98
Anacortes, WA 98221
(888) 448-4862
www.clearsnap.com
· Style Stones, MicaMagic, inks,
 stamps and stamping supplies

JudiKins
17803 Harvard Boulevard
Gardena, CA 90248
(310) 515-1115
www.judikins.com
· Diamond Glaze, shrink plastic,
 stamps and stamping supplies

The Leather Factory
www.leatherfactory.com
· Leather, tools and findings

Loose Ends
2065 Madrona Avenue Southeast
Salem, OR 97302
(866) 390-2348
www.looseends.com
· Handmade papers and
 tin garlands

Papers by Catherine
11328 S. Post Oak Road, #108
Houston, TX 77035
(713) 723-3334
www.papersbycatherine.com
· Handmade and decorative papers

Plaid Enterprises
3225 Westech
Norcross, GA 30092
(800) 842-4197
www.plaidonline.com
· Acrylic paints, stamps
 and supplies

Polyform Products Co.
1901 Estes Ave.
Elk Grove Village, IL 60007
www.sculpey.com
· Polymer clay, tools and materials

Prairie Craft Company
P.O. Box 209
Florissant, CO 80816-0209
(800) 779-0615
www.prairiecraft.com
· Kato Polyclay and polymer
 clay products

Ranger Industries
15 Park Road
Tinton Falls, NJ 07724
(732) 389-3535
www.rangerink.com
· Inkpads, embossing powders
 and heat embossing tools

Staedtler Inc.
21900 Plummer St.
Chatsworth, CA 91311
www.staedtler.com
· Crayons, markers and
 cutting mats

**Suze Weinberg Design
Studio, Inc.**
11 Bannard Street
Freehold, NJ 07728
(732) 761-2400
www.schmoozewithsuze.com
· Ultra Thick embossing enamel
 and stamping supplies

Tsukineko
17640 North East 65th Street
Redmond, WA 98052
(425) 883-7733
www.tsukineko.com
· Pens and inks

USArtQuest, Inc.
7800 Ann Arbor Road
Grass Lake, MI 49240
(517) 522-6225
www.usartquest.com
· Perfect Paper Adhesive

VIP
1215 N. Grove St.
Anaheim, CA 92806
· Foils and spray webbing

Woodworks Ltd.
4521 Anderson Boulevard
Fort Worth, TX 76117
(817) 581-5230
www.craftparts.com
· Wooden beads

STAMP COMPANIES

A Stamp in the Hand **(310) 884-9700,** www.astampinthehand.com

Acey-Deucy **(518) 398-5108,** www.stampdiva.com/aceydeucy.html

American Art Stamp **(310) 371-6593,** www.americanartstamp.com

Anima Designs **(412) 726-8401,** www.animadesigns.com

Black Cat Designs **(07) 3865-8066,** www.thestamptrap.com.au

Claudia Rose **(845) 679-9235,** www.claudiarose.com

DeNami Design **(253) 437-1626,** www.denamidesign.com

Ducks in a Row **(408) 378-2677,** www.ducksinarowrs.com

ERA Graphics **(530) 344-9322,** www.eragraphics.com

Hero Arts **(510) 652-6055,** www.heroarts.com

Impress Me Rubber Stamps **(818) 788-6730,** www.impressmenow.com

Inkadinkado Rubber Stamps **(610) 939-9900,** www.inkadinkado.com

JudiKins **(310) 515-1115,** www.judikins.com

Magenta Rubber Stamps **(450) 922-5253,** www.magentastyle.com

Paper Parachute **(503) 533-4513,** www.paperparachute.com

Personal Stamp Exchange (PSX) **(559) 294-4444,** www.duncancrafts.com

Picture Show P.O. Box 65440, St. Paul, MN 55165

Posh Impressions **(800) 421-7674,** www.poshimpressions.com

Postmodern Design **(405) 321-3716**

Rubber Monger **(928) 536-5128,** www.rubbermonger.com

Rubber Moon **(208) 772-9772,** www.rubbermoon.com

Rubber Stampede **(562) 695-7969,** www.deltacrafts.com

Stamp Oasis **(702) 880-8886,** www.stampoasis.com

Stampendous! **(714) 688-0288,** www.stampendous.com

Stampington & Company **(949) 380-7318,** www.stampington.com

Stampers Anonymous **(800) 945-3980,** www.stampersanonymous.com

Stampotique Originals **(602) 862-0237,** www.stampotique.com

Stephanie Olin Designs **(714) 848-1227,** www.stephanieolin.com

Time to Stamp **(951) 845-9242,** www.timetostamp.com

Uptown Design Company **(253) 925-1234,** www.uptowndesign.com

Zettiology **(253) 638-6466,** www.zettiology.com

And check out my new DVD!

Fabricadabra: Material Magic with Sandra McCall
PageSage
580 Crespi Drive, #A6-216
Pacifica, CA 94044
www.pagesage.com

INDEX

THE BEST STAMPING AND JEWELRY BOOKS COME FROM NORTH LIGHT BOOKS!

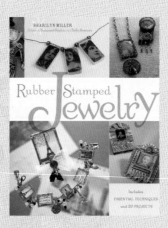

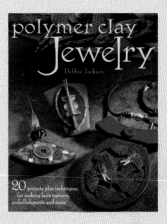

30-Minute Rubber Stamp Workshop

Sandra McCall

Create a wonderful, personal gift in the time it takes to drive to the store! Sandra McCall will show you how. This must-have book features 30 quick and easy projects, including 11 wearable gifts such as pins, necklaces and bracelets. Through full color illustration and clear, step-by-step instructions, you'll be making wonderful creations in no time!

128 pages   #32142-K
ISBN 1-58180-271-4 $24.99

Making Gifts with Rubber Stamps

Sandra McCall

Sandra McCall shows you how to make unique, expressive gifts by stamping in polymer clay, shrink plastic and handmade paper.

128 pages   #31667-K
ISBN 1-58180-081-9 $22.99

Rubber Stamped Jewelry

Sharilyn Miller

This book combines the self-expressive qualities of rubber stamping with the elegance of jewelry making. Through easy-to-follow instructions and beautiful full-color photos, Sharilyn Miller provides tips and techniques for creating earrings, necklaces, bracelets and brooches using a wide array of materials including fabric, shrink plastic and more. The book also includes 20 projects from the author and contributing artists.

128 pages   #32415-K
ISBN 1-58180-384-2 $22.99

Polymer Clay Jewelry

Debbie Jackson

Learn to create 20 gorgeous projects with an array of polymer clay and jewelry-making techniques. Debbie Jackson shows you how to use embellishments, textures, liquid polymer clay and canes to create one-of-a-kind pieces that will dazzle your friends and loved ones.

128 pages   #32873-K
ISBN 1-58180-513-6 $22.99

These and other fine North Light titles are available from your local art and craft retailer, bookstore, online supplier or by calling 1-800-448-0915.